Michel de Montaigne, Lizzie Eliza Rector

The education of children

Michel de Montaigne, Lizzie Eliza Rector
The education of children
ISBN/EAN: 9783337215453

Printed in Europe, USA, Canada, Australia, Japan

Cover: Foto ©Paul-Georg Meister /pixelio.de

More available books at **www.hansebooks.com**

International Education Series

EDITED BY
WILLIAM T. HARRIS, A. M., LL. D.

Volume XLVI

INTERNATIONAL EDUCATION SERIES.

12mo, cloth, uniform binding.

THE INTERNATIONAL EDUCATION SERIES was projected for the purpose of bringing together in orderly arrangement the best writings, new and old, upon educational subjects, and presenting a complete course of reading and training for teachers generally. It is edited by WILLIAM T. HARRIS, LL. D., United States Commissioner of Education, who has contributed for the different volumes in the way of introduction, analysis, and commentary. The volumes are tastefully and substantially bound in uniform style.

VOLUMES NOW READY.

1. **The Philosophy of Education.** By JOHANN K. F. ROSENKRANZ, Doctor of Theology and Professor of Philosophy, University of Königsberg. Translated by ANNA C. BRACKETT. Second edition, revised, with Commentary and complete Analysis. $1.50.

2. **A History of Education.** By F. V. N. PAINTER, A. M., Professor of Modern Languages and Literature, Roanoke College, Va. $1.50.

3. **The Rise and Early Constitution of Universities.** WITH A SURVEY OF MEDIÆVAL EDUCATION. By S. S. LAURIE, LL. D., Professor of the Institutes and History of Education, University of Edinburgh. $1.50.

4. **The Ventilation and Warming of School Buildings.** By GILBERT B. MORRISON, Teacher of Physics and Chemistry, Kansas City High School. $1.00.

5. **The Education of Man.** By FRIEDRICH FROEBEL. Translated and annotated by W. N. HAILMANN, A. M., Superintendent of Public Schools, La Porte, Ind. $1.50.

6. **Elementary Psychology and Education.** By JOSEPH BALDWIN, A. M., LL. D., author of "The Art of School Management." $1.50.

7. **The Senses and the Will.** (Part I of "THE MIND OF THE CHILD.") By W. PREYER, Professor of Physiology in Jena. Translated by H. W. BROWN, Teacher in the State Normal School at Worcester, Mass. $1.50.

8. **Memory: What it is and How to Improve it.** By DAVID KAY, F. R. G. S., author of "Education and Educators," etc. $1.50.

9. **The Development of the Intellect.** (Part II of "THE MIND OF THE CHILD.") By W. PREYER, Professor of Physiology in Jena. Translated by H. W. BROWN. $1.50.

10. **How to Study Geography.** A Practical Exposition of Methods and Devices in Teaching Geography which apply the Principles and Plans of Ritter and Guyot. By FRANCIS W. PARKER, Principal of the Cook County (Illinois) Normal School. $1.50.

11. **Education in the United States: Its History from the Earliest Settlements.** By RICHARD G. BOONE, A. M., Professor of Pedagogy, Indiana University. $1.50.

12. **European Schools;** or, WHAT I SAW IN THE SCHOOLS OF GERMANY, FRANCE, AUSTRIA, AND SWITZERLAND. By L. R. KLEMM, Ph. D., Principal of the Cincinnati Technical School. Fully illustrated. $2.00.

13. **Practical Hints for the Teachers of Public Schools.** By GEORGE HOWLAND, Superintendent of the Chicago Public Schools. $1.00.

14. **Pestalozzi: His Life and Work.** By ROGER DE GUIMPS. Authorized Translation from the second French edition, by J. RUSSELL, B. A. With an Introduction by Rev. R. H. QUICK, M. A. $1.50.

15. **School Supervision.** By J. L. PICKARD, LL. D. $1.00.

16. **Higher Education of Women in Europe.** By HELENE LANGE, Berlin. Translated and accompanied by comparative statistics by L. R. KLEMM. $1.00.

17. **Essays on Educational Reformers.** By ROBERT HERBERT QUICK, M. A., Trinity College, Cambridge. Only authorized edition of the work as rewritten in 1890. $1.50.

18. **A Text-Book in Psychology.** By JOHANN FRIEDRICH HERBART. Translated by MARGARET K. SMITH. $1.00.

THE INTERNATIONAL EDUCATION SERIES.—(Continued.)

19. **Psychology Applied to the Art of Teaching.** By JOSEPH BALDWIN, A. M., LL. D. $1.50.
20. **Rousseau's Émile; or, Treatise on Education.** Translated and annotated by W. H. PAYNE, Ph. D., LL. D. $1.50.
21. **The Moral Instruction of Children.** By FELIX ADLER. $1.50.
22. **English Education in the Elementary and Secondary Schools.** By ISAAC SHARPLESS, LL. D., President of Haverford College. $1.00.
23. **Education from a National Standpoint.** By ALFRED FOUILLÉE. $1.50.
24. **Mental Development of the Child.** By W. PREYER, Professor of Physiology in Jena. Translated by H. W. BROWN. $1.00.
25. **How to Study and Teach History.** By B. A. HINSDALE, Ph. D., LL. D., University of Michigan. $1.50.
26. **Symbolic Education.** A COMMENTARY ON FROEBEL's "MOTHER-PLAY." By SUSAN E. BLOW. $1.50.
27. **Systematic Science Teaching.** By EDWARD GARDNIER HOWE. $1.50.
28. **The Education of the Greek People.** By THOMAS DAVIDSON. $1.50.
29. **The Evolution of the Massachusetts Public-School System.** By G. H. MARTIN, A. M. $1.50.
30. **Pedagogics of the Kindergarten.** By FRIEDRICH FROEBEL. 12mo. $1.50.
31. **The Mottoes and Commentaries of Freidrich Froebel's Mother-Play.** By SUSAN E. BLOW and HENRIETTA R. ELIOT. $1.50.
32. **The Songs and Music of Froebel's Mother-Play.** By SUSAN E. BLOW. $1.50.
33. **The Psychology of Number, and its Application to Methods of Teaching Arithmetic.** By JAMES A. MCLELLAN, A. M., and JOHN DEWEY, Ph. D. $1.50.
34. **Teaching the Language-Arts.** SPEECH, READING, COMPOSITION. By B. A. HINSDALE, Ph. D., LL. D. $1.00.
35. **The Intellectual and Moral Development of the Child.** PART I. Containing Chapters on PERCEPTION, EMOTION, MEMORY, IMAGINATION, and CONSCIOUSNESS. By GABRIEL COMPAYRÉ. Translated from the French by MARY E. WILSON. $1.50.
36. **Herbart's A B C of Sense-Perception, and Introductory Works.** By WILLIAM J. ECKOFF, Ph. D., PD. D. $1.50.
37. **Psychologic Foundations of Education.** By WILLIAM T. HARRIS, A. M., LL. D. $1.50.
38. **The School System of Ontario.** By the Hon. GEORGE W. ROSS, LL. D., Minister of Education for the Province of Ontario. $1.00.
39. **Principles and Practice of Teaching.** By JAMES JOHONNOT. $1.50.
40. **School Management and School Methods.** By JOSEPH BALDWIN. $1.50.
41. **Froebel's Educational Laws for all Teachers.** By JAMES L. HUGHES, Inspector of Schools, Toronto. $1.50.
42. **Bibliography of Education.** By WILL S. MONROE, A. B. $2.00.
43. **The Study of the Child.** By A. R. TAYLOR, Ph. D. $1.50.
44. **Education by Development.** By FRIEDRICH FROEBEL. Translated by JOSEPHINE JARVIS. $1.50.
45. **Letters to a Mother.** By SUSAN E. BLOW. $1.50.
46. **Montaigne's Education of the Child.** Translated by L. E. RECTOR. $1.00.

OTHER VOLUMES IN PREPARATION.

D. APPLETON AND COMPANY, NEW YORK.

INTERNATIONAL EDUCATION SERIES

MONTAIGNE
THE EDUCATION OF CHILDREN

SELECTED, TRANSLATED, AND ANNOTATED

BY

L. E. RECTOR, Pd. D.

NEW YORK
D. APPLETON AND COMPANY
1899

Reproduced by
DUOPAGE PROCESS
in the
U.S. of America

Micro Photo Division
Bell & Howell Company
Cleveland 12, Ohio

COPYRIGHT, 1899,
BY D. APPLETON AND COMPANY.

ELECTROTYPED AND PRINTED
AT THE APPLETON PRESS, U. S. A.

EDITOR'S PREFACE.

The significance of Montaigne lies chiefly in his protest against pedantry. Learning is a good thing when what is learned consists of the wisdom of the past, and when what is learned is assimilated and made useful to solve the problems that press for a solution in our own age. An undigested accumulation of scraps of learning is not of practical use. It never helps the scholar to think nor enables him to act, nor to guide the action of others.

The accumulation of knowledge that is not systematized in itself nor applied to the solution of practical problems is to be shunned. The display of such knowledge is pedantry.

It is true, however, that man without any knowledge of the development of his race remains at the bottom of the ladder which his ancestors have built for him. He can not enter into the heritage of what his ancestors have discovered for him by painful experience. Ancient literatures are full of knowledge of human nature, and they show methods of avoiding errors. But for him—the illiterate man—their solutions do not exist. All the more must he follow the customs and usages of his parents and neighbours. Not knowing the origin of these customs he must observe superstitiously all the punctilios without variation. He can not make adaptations of his knowledge to the actual conditions of his work. But the man of science can reconstruct his manners and customs, modifying them to suit circumstances. For he can follow the spirit of the accumulated wisdom. He can understand principles, and is far more practical than the man who merely knows the use and wont of his time.

Learning, then, is a prime necessity. The danger of an accumulation of useless learning and of a pedantic display of it is a secondary matter, and must always remain secondary. But although secondary it is a very pathetic circumstance connected with education. Yet it is more pathetic to see human beings entirely deprived of a share of the knowledge of literature and science and experience of human life. To see the remedy for darkness so managed as to create no life in the soul—to see wisdom turned into pedantry—is the next most pathetic thing in education.

The educational reformer in his indignation forgets that there are some sturdy souls among the pupils who can find nourishment in the driest and dullest scholastic presentation. The school justifies itself by its use to these sturdy souls who nourish their originality upon the erudition which quite crushes out the self-activity of their feebler fellow-pupils.

One may sum up the literature of the educational reformers by saying that it condemns the existing system of education because its methods are calculated to cram the pupil's memory instead of educating his judgment, and to teach artificial formalities instead of natural modes of action, and, besides, are careless of his physical well-being and of his usefulness to his environment. These reformers, in fact, get so impatient with the faults in method of instruction that they one and all condemn, in moments of excitement, the learning which the schools profess to teach. Even if it is the wisdom of the race, they pronounce it useless to the pupil.

In dealing with the parts of this problem Rabelais laid stress on comparing and verifying ancient knowledge by applying it to the objects of one's experience. Montaigne attacked pedantry. Comenius sought to unite the pupil's practical activity with his theoretical: "Learn to do by doing." Locke laid particular stress on the health of the body, and he placed in the foreground the cultivation of sense-perception. Rousseau wished to do away with all artificial manners and customs and return to what he called a state of nature. Pestalozzi followed Locke in accentuating the importance of sense-perception. Friedrich Froebel carried the doctrine of self-activity to the minutest details of education, making the child begin at the very first with assimilating what is taught him, and making him rediscover by his own investigation the successive steps of learning.

Montaigne stands for very much more as a literary man than as an educational reformer. He is called by Emerson in his Representative Men "The Sceptic." By "sceptic" he means that Montaigne recognizes the good of the existing order, but at the same time sees the objections to it. "Scepticism is the attitude assumed by the student in relation to the particulars which society adores, but which he sees to be reverend only in their tendency and spirit."

Montaigne's motto is, What do I know?— *Que sçais je?* He disparages memory and says harsh things about words, preferring things to words. In his protest he goes so far as to despise civilization and prefer a condition of war, such as we find among barbarous nations, to arts and letters. He praises the Spartans over the Athenians. While he condemns books and words and learning, he gives us in his essays one of the most remarkable examples of the scholarly use of learning. But he carries his habit of quoting from classical writers to the extreme. In fact, according to our recent standards of literary style, his quotations are so numerous that they make his style pedantic.

Like all educational reformers, he not only attacks the methods of education which do not develop the pupil's self-activity, but he condemns, as before said, books and learning, arts and letters themselves. It always amuses one to see a man declaiming against books by writing a new book in order to condemn books. Education ought to teach the pupil how to escape the slavery to books and the slavery to authority and custom. The pupil should be educated above all blind obedience to what is prescribed by external authority. But all education deals with prescription, on the one hand, and hence as soon as education begins to educate it begins to set the pupil to the serious task of learning what others have taught. Of course, too, we shall find, if we seize the process of education as it is going on, that the pupil in his effort to master the wisdom of others holds in his mind scraps of this wisdom in all degrees of assimilation. Some of it he already understands very well, and has made it his own. He can think with it, act with it, and solve the problem of life with it. Other material he has not quite grasped, although he has considerable insight into it. Still other parts of what he is learning are in a state of being seized upon by his mind. He finds them expressed in words. He has seized the words and is trying to put meaning into them, but has not yet succeeded.

The stomach of the feeding animal contains elements of food in all stages of the process of digestion. It is easy to condemn the work of the school by discovering and describing that part of it which is in the process of seizing the words, and which has not yet been elaborated by the pupil sufficiently to convert it into thought and action. The good school, alike with the poor school, would suffer by such a method of criticism. Much harm is done by this indiscriminate condemnation of the work of the school and by the wholesale charge of pedantry based upon that part of its studies which is contained in the beginning of the process, and not in its later stages or the completed result.

Doubtless schools fail so often in taking their pupils beyond this initiatory process in which they get the words but do not yet master their meaning, nor see their application to thought and action, that this wholesale criticism has a strong case. For the actual work of teaching, making as its main object the instruction of the pupil in a branch of learning— leading him to its mastery, first, by the seizing of the words and discovering their meaning, and finally making a practical application of them, may injure the pupil's health, may overload his memory, or cause him to be careless in the use of his sense-perception. It may overwork or underwork any phase of the body or of the mind. It is in his effort to startle the educator and arouse him to the importance of avoiding these errors that Montaigne sometimes attacks knowledge itself, and even the desire for mental cultivation.

Ignorance is often betrayed regarding the value of learning to know language by eye as well as by ear. Skilful and accurate thinking comes from a knowledge of language addressed to the eye in the form of printed or written words. A knowledge of language by the ear does not extend much beyond the colloquial vocabulary, and is insufficient for the expression of accurate observation or scientific thought. And yet while a tirade is made against letters in one place, in another place the reformer inconsistently betrays his great respect for a speaking and writing knowledge of Latin. Does not Montaigne himself pride himself on the method of instruction which his father gave him, by which he learned to speak Latin from his tutor even in infancy?

Rabelais, too, makes Cicero his ideal model of learning, and requires his pupil to be so well acquainted with Cicero's Latin that he expresses himself with proper gestures, distinct pronunciation, persuasive voice, and in Ciceronian Latin.

Rabelais's idea of a course of instruction for his giant pupil requires him first of all to learn the languages perfectly—Greek, Latin, Hebrew, Chaldee, and Arabic. He wishes the pupil to form his style on the Greek of Plato and his Latin style on Cicero. Besides these languages he prescribes history and geography, geometry, arithmetic, music, and astronomy. He wishes him to master the civil law, and to know botany, zoology, and mineralogy, besides the Greek and Arabian medical lore, and the Talmud and Cabala.

Montaigne in another place attacks poetry, apparently seeing only some of its superficial influences upon the mind. He does not see, as the theory of education in our days sees, that the great poets are the great revealers of human nature, and that they understand the motives of human action and give the pupil who reads their great works of art the most valuable of all knowledge—namely, a knowledge of human nature.

Montaigne is a tonic or a sort of corrective against pedantry. But he is confused in his judgments as to what is really valuable in education. In fact he does not see the real province of the school. His preference of the Spartans to the Athenians, of the savage tribe to the civilized nation, and of Plutarch to the great national poets, all show this. And yet he does not overestimate the value of Plutarch; he simply underestimates the value of the national poetry.

In her admirable "Story of a Short Life" Mrs. Horatio Ewing shows how a lame soul may be cured. No one of Montaigne's essays could bring such a lesson to a lame soul; though his maxims are a sovereign cure for pedantry and useless knowledge. But when he decries knowledge and praises accomplishments he overestimates skill in the management of particular things. Goethe's maxim should be remembered as far saner than Montaigne's: "Baked bread is good and sufficient for the day, but seed corn should not be ground." Perhaps, however, Goethe borrowed from Montaigne or Rabelais his idea that the most important species of education is that which takes place by means of error. He says that it is not the part of the teacher to hold the child back from error, but to teach him by means of his error. To have the child learn by error seems to resemble that doctrine which has become quite popular within the last few years—namely, to have the child pass through the culture epochs of the human race in his common-school course. It is obvious, moreover, that the method must be used very sparingly, and the unseen providence of the teacher must watch over the pupil and prevent fatal mistakes.

Montaigne, then, will be read with most profit by those teachers whose chief fault is pedantry—who, in short, are satisfied best when their pupils learn the most by what is called the cramming process. It is necessary, however, to caution that class of teachers against the reliability of Montaigne's opinions on historic events and characters. For although Montaigne declaims furiously against pedantry, yet perhaps the majority of his judgments have no other than a pedantic basis. For example, he borrows Cicero's opinion of Cæsar's ambition. It is a view of Cæsar which has been a favourite of the schoolmasters of all times. But it is pedantry not to see the great and serious deed of Cæsar, who strove to give the freedom of Roman law to the peoples of the world living outside of Italy. Cæsar inaugurated the modern world by bringing the neighbouring nations of Europe within the Roman Empire and putting them to school to learn Roman law and civil rights. The Roman republic stood directly across the path to this great step in world history.

The selfish aristocracy of the Roman senate, whose ideal of government was to place the foot of their tyranny on the neck of the human race, had to be displaced by a one-man power, which made itself strong by the armies in the field and which looked toward a wise administration of distant provinces rather than toward a selfish oppression of those provinces for the benefit of the people of Italy. The Roman senate would not permit foreign provinces to be managed for their own good. It was Cæsar and not the Roman senate who worked for the freedom of the world. But Cicero could not see this, nor do the Ciceronian disciples found among our modern schoolmasters.

W. T. HARRIS.

WASHINGTON, D. C., *June 10, 1899.*

AUTHOR'S PREFACE.

Compayré, in his Histoire de la Pédagogie, says that before pretending to surpass the theories of Erasmus, Rabelais, and Montaigne, we of this day should rather attempt to overtake them and to equal them in most of their pedagogical precepts. "Montaigne may be said to have founded a school of thinkers on the subject of education, of which Locke and Rousseau were afterward the great exponents," is the opinion of Mr. Quick in his Educational Reformers. Notwithstanding Montaigne's undoubted influence and the fact that Essays XXIV and XXV of the First Book have become classical in education, we have yet to record one more proof that " all books on education are printed in German." Reimer's Michael von Montaigne: Ansichten über die Erziehung der Kinder, in the Pädagogische Bibliothek, has remained a challenge for English and American educators since 1875.

In making my translation I have followed

the edition of Courbet and Royer (5 vols., Paris, 1873-91), based upon the variorum edition of 1854 (Paris, 4 vols.). Wherever possible the translation has been compared with the text of the original edition of 1580, which consisted of the first two books only. I have not hesitated, however, to use the rendering of the 1603 Florio, and of the 1842 Cotton, whenever such rendering seemed preferable to my own. To the latter especially am I indebted for the metrical translation of many of the numerous quotations.

The English reader, who desires a more detailed account of Montaigne's life than I have given, is referred to Bayle St. John's delightful Montaigne the Essayist (London, 1858). The French reader will find vast stores of information in the exhaustive studies of M. Grün and Dr. Payen.

Perhaps it should be here stated that in 1893 Dr. MacAlister "set out to edit with introduction and notes such portions of Montaigne's Essays as relates to education." Pressure of other duties compelled Dr. MacAlister to defer the work, but it is needless to say that no one will welcome his Montaigne more cordially than the editor of the present volume.

L. E. RECTOR.

CONTENTS.

	PAGE
EDITOR'S PREFACE	iii–xiv
AUTHOR'S PREFACE	xv, xvi
CONTENTS	xvii
TOPICAL ANALYSIS	xix–xxiii
INTRODUCTION	1–18
Biographical	1–6
Critical	7–12
Montaigne, Locke, and Rousseau	13–17
Some modern educational ideas anticipated by Montaigne	18
TRANSLATIONS	19–152
Of the education of children, Book i, chapter xxv	19–85
Of pedantry, Book i, chapter xxiv	86–109
Of the affection of fathers to their children, Book ii, chapter viii	110–120
Of liars, Book i, chapter ix	121, 122
Book ii, chapter xviii	122, 123
Of habit, Book i, chapter xxii	124–126
Of presumption, Book ii, chapter xvii	127–129
Of physiognomy, Book iii, chapter xii	130–133
Of anger, Book ii, chapter xxxi	134–137
Of the art of conversation, Book iii, chapter viii	138–140
Of idleness, Book i, chapter viii	141, 142
Of experience, Book iii, chapter xiii	143–146
History, Book ii, chapter x; i, xvi; i, xx	147–152
NOTES	153–170
INDEX OF NAMES	171–178
GENERAL INDEX	179–191

TOPICAL ANALYSIS.

	PAGE
Introduction—Biographical	1–6
Montaigne born at Périgord, 1533	1
Importance of his family	1
Pierre Eyquem and his ideas of education	2
Early influences from Italy, Pau, and from Rabelais	2
Leaves college and studies law	2
Becomes *conseiller*, 1557; mayor 1581	3
Forms friendship with Estienne de la Boëtie	3
Marriage in 1565	4
Travels in Italy, Switzerland, and Germany	4
Translates Sebonde's Theologia Naturalis	4
Montaigne's attitude on the subject of religion	5
Montaigne's last days and death in 1592	6
Introduction—Critical	7–12
Requirements of modern education	7
Montaigne's relation to these requirements	7, 8
Narrowing effect of teaching	8
Life *versus* systems	9
Montaigne's denunciation of inflexibility	9
Every age presents panaceas for ills of mankind	10
Montaigne's order of studies	10, 11
Decoration of schoolrooms anticipated by Montaigne	11
Relation of method to instruction	11
Montaigne places emphasis upon individuality	12
Introduction—Montaigne, Locke, and Rousseau	13–17
Montaigne charged with lacking in originality	13
Montaigne first to develop educational ideas	13
Coste and Quick admit Locke's debt to Montaigne	13

	PAGE
Dependence of Locke and Rousseau upon Montaigne shown under following points:	
1. Choice of tutor	15
2. Use of motor side in educational games	15
3. Train for practical life	17
6. Importance of history	17
7. Character most important	17
3. Importance of physical training	16
4. Condemns harsh methods—school life should be made pleasant	16
Of the education of children	19–85
Montaigne's intellectual limitations	19
His opinions coincide with those of other writers	21
Chrysippus and Epicurus compared	22
Quotations often bring out an author's weakness	23
Montaigne introduces his subject of education	24
Relation of children's early inclinations to their education	24
Education of especial value to those of noble birth	26
Choice of tutor all-important	27
Child study	29
Individual teaching favoured	29
Apperception and Herbartian co-ordination	29
Dogmatism illustrated	30
Pupil's own judgment should be cultivated	31
Borrowed matter to be assimilated	32
Apperception not mere memorizing	33
Travel of great importance	34
Parents should not spoil their children	35
Importance of physical training	36
Home influence often interferes with the child's training	37
"Children should be seen, not heard"	37
Only great minds should assume unusual privileges	38
Train pupils to be fair in argument	39
Patriotism inculcated	39
Errors should be frankly acknowledged	40
General observation of great value	41
Scope of history	42
Broadening influence of travel	44
The world the best text-book	46

TOPICAL ANALYSIS.

xxi

	PAGE
Pythagoras compares life to the Olympic games	47
Relation of philosophical examples to life	47
Train for practical life	48
Useless knowledge	49
Method of instruction	50
Study should not be made difficult	51
The practice of virtue is pleasurable	54
Office of true virtue	54
Children to be educated according to their ability	56
Philosophy adapted to early instruction	56
Aristotle's training of Alexander	57
Danger of too much book study	58
Philosophy in its relation to life the chief study	59
The whole man should be trained	60
Study to be made pleasant, but effeminacy avoided	61
College discipline too rigorous	62
Make school life pleasant	62
Singularity of manners to be avoided	63
Cultivate adaptability	64
Learn to live	66
"Actions speak louder than words"	67
Pedantry ridiculed	68
Things before words	68
Invention the test of true poetry	72
Sophistical subtleties unworthy of serious attention	72
Style and matter should harmonize	73
Avoid affectation in dress and language	74
Imitation of words easy, of thoughts difficult	76
Vernacular first	76
Montaigne's early education	77
Use of motor side	79
Montaigne's disposition accounts for partial failure of this educational scheme	80
The tale the best literature for children	81
Montaigne's inaction	82
Montaigne approves of the stage	84
Learning should be made alluring and permanent	85
Of pedantry	86–100
Pedantry despised by ancients and moderns	86

THE EDUCATION OF CHILDREN.

	PAGE
Ability *versus* mere learning and material circumstances	88
Ancient and modern pedants contrasted	89
True philosophers are great in action	90
Some philosophers who refused public office	90
The better learned preferable to the more learned	91
Pedants neglect moral training	92
Pupils no better than the pedants	93
Buying brains	94
No learning of use but what we make our own	95
Schools furnish children with little real knowledge	96
Pretenders to learning	97
A pedant ridiculed	98
Pedants have little judgment	99
Women require little learning	101
Some more fit for business than for the pursuit of knowledge	102
People may apply learning to evil	103
Persian system of education	104
Cyrus whipped for an unjust decision	105
Athenian and Spartan systems of education contrasted	106
The least learned nation the most warlike	108
Of the affection of fathers to their children	110–120
Montaigne considers his subject unique	110
Madame D'Estissac extolled as a good mother	111
Gratitude due her from her son	111
Paternal affection is greater than filial	112
Children's rights	113
A father should be respected for himself, not for his money	115
Physical violence condemned	116
Parents and children should be friends	117
Mistake of Marshal de Montluc	118
Children should be somewhat familiar with their parents	120
Of liars	121–123
Children should be trained to speak the truth	121
Falsehood the beginning of corruption	122
A lie is contemptible	123
Of habit	124–126
Plato on habit	124
Parents to blame for not correcting childish vices	124

TOPICAL ANALYSIS. xxiii

	PAGE
Plays of children of great importance	125
Of presumption	127-129
Formal education condemned	127
Every one susceptible to instruction	128
Education reformatory	128
Vernacular suited to philosophy	129
Of physiognomy	130-133
Simplicity commended	130
Intemperance in letters	131
Little learning needed to live well	132
Of anger	134-137
Children should be educated by the State	134
Parents who punish their children often injure them	135
Anger perverts justice	136
The art of conversation	138-140
Learning does not teach effective expression	138
Knowledge useless which does not improve the mind	139
Of idleness	141-142
Mind requires occupation	141
Of experience	143-146
Go back to Nature for wisdom	143
Children should be trained to like ordinary things	144
Children should not be brought up in luxury	145
History	147-152
History best taught by biography	147
Plutarch	147
Cæsar	148
Classes of historians—Froissart	149
An eye-witness the best historian	150
Value of history relative to the author	151
Clergymen and philosophers should not write history	152

MONTAIGNE'S VIEWS ON THE EDUCATION OF CHILDREN.

INTRODUCTION.

BIOGRAPHICAL.

MICHEL EYQUEM, lord of Montaigne, was born in Périgord, a province of Guyenne, in 1533. His family was an important one in western France, and Montaigne had good reason to be proud of his lineage. As far back as the time of the Black Prince we find Eyquem mentioned, and it is not an uncommon name in France even at present. This consideration of family is of interest to the student of education only in so far as it serves to throw light on Montaigne's own character and educational opinions. Like John Locke, he never for a moment ceased to remember that he belonged to a privileged class.

An account of the early life and training of Montaigne may be found in the essay Concerning the Education of Children (page 77 et seq.). This experiment in education had its origin in a peculiar combination of circumstances. The father, Pierre Eyquem, visited Florence and Rome in his fighting days, during what the French call the discovery of Italy, and received a strong intellectual impulse. At this time, also, Marguerite de Navarre was at Pau, the centre of a little court of learned, wise, and imaginative men. Many of these scholars, on their way to and from Paris, were entertained at Montaigne, and discoursed with the lord of the castle opinions literary, political, and educational. One other influence must be considered—Rabelais's Chronique Gargantuine was given to the world in 1532, the Pantagruel a few months later. These three streams of influence emanating from Italy, Pau, and from the Comic Homer, produced theories ready to be poured upon the boy born in 1533. They overflowed upon the early treatment of Henry IV and others of this period—so full of thirst for novelty—as is shown by biographies of noted men living during the latter part of the sixteenth century.

Soon after leaving college, at the early age of thirteen, Montaigne tells us he was plunged over head and ears in law. Where he studied, and for what period, is left to conjecture. His father had been an important member of the government of Bordeaux, and was anxious that his son should wear the red robe of *conseiller* to the parliament of that city. The essayist attained the honour in 1557, and in 1581 was even elected mayor. Notwithstanding these positions, Montaigne never showed any great proficiency as a legal student, nor was he remarkable in any way as an executive. The experience, however, served to broaden the man of the world, and gave him an insight into governmental affairs that shows all through the Essays. Whatever we may think of public life, either in our own time or in the sixteenth century, we must give the politician credit for a knowledge of human nature which is possessed by few persons of other callings.

While *conseiller* he became acquainted with Estienne de la Boëtie, the author of Voluntary Servitude, a little tract embodying the best of the revolutionary movement of his time. We find traces of La Boëtie in Milton, in Rousseau, and in Lamennais. The warm friendship which sprang up between the two men helped to develop Montaigne's mind, gave a tone to his writings, and touched his nature with a refinement it might otherwise have lacked. Many things which appear inconsistent when we compare Montaigne's environment on the one hand, and his words on the other, may be explained by this classical friendship. Under the influence of La Boëtie, Montaigne becomes less the cautious lover of compromise and more the champion of fair play in politics, religion, and education.

Until his marriage in 1565 to Françoise de la Chassagne, the essayist seems to have followed the practices of most young men of his century. He visited Paris, remaining months at a time; was successively honoured by Catherine de Medici, Francis II, Charles IX, and Henry III. He became a soldier, would spend a few weeks with the army and return home. Previous to his election as mayor of Bordeaux, Montaigne spent two years in travel, and has left us a most delightful picture of Italy, Switzerland, and southern Germany during the latter half of the sixteenth century. While at Rome "The Maestro del Sacro Palasso returned to me my Essays marked with the *expurgata;* among these was the essay On the Education of Children," an interesting commentary on the time.

As a young man Montaigne had translated for "the best father that ever lived" a book by Ramondus de Sebonde, called Theologia Naturalis, which undertook by human and natural reasons to establish against the atheists all the articles of the Christian religion. This work gave to Montaigne's mind and language a pietistic hue which they never quite lost, and possibly did something toward throwing him into that state of uncertainty from which he never recovered. His attitude on the subject of religion was the distinctively modern one. While he adhered to the older form of Christianity, he saw no reason why Protestants and Catholics should not live side by side, as he did with his brother Beauregard, who had joined the Calvinists. In this connection it is worth noting that dogma and bigotry have never made a contribution to educational thought. Much of the greatness of Greece may be attributed to her wonderful freedom in religious matters, a fact which has not received due importance in histories of education. The great teachers have been men of religious feeling, never bigots, and Montaigne was no exception in this regard. Remember, too, this was the century of St. Bartholomew. Montaigne's moderation was shown also during the civil wars, which produced such frightful disorder. "Among so many armed houses, I am the only man I know, in France, who has confided purely to Heaven." Few can comport themselves with a complacency so entire, and yet it is this spirit in the man which gives us such confidence in his opinions. Here is one who has seen everything, experienced everything, is intimate with the cruel ways of the human heart, and yet he believes that underneath all this tragedy man is teachable and worthy of every effort. The paradox of existence no writer has realized more keenly, lived it more manfully, and expressed it so clearly.

The manner of his death was not inconsistent with his life. Realizing that his end was near, he paid those to whom he had left legacies the amount in money, and then requested his wife to send for certain gentlemen to whom he wished to say farewell. When they had arrived, just as the priest was elevating the Host, "This poor gentleman," says Pasquier, "leaped forward as well as he was able on the bed, with his hands clasped, and in this last act gave up his soul to God, which was a fine mirror of the interior of his mind." He was buried at Montaigne; afterward the body was removed to the vault of the University buildings at Bordeaux, where it now rests.

CRITICAL.

In a broad, general way civilized countries at the present time agree as to the purpose of a child's school life. There must be: (1) Such training of the body as shall fit it for the demands made upon it; (2) acquisition of knowledge; (3) training for usefulness; (4) training for enjoyment; (5) development of character. The means by which these results are to be attained are also a matter of agreement. (1) By placing a child in relation with his human environment by means of literature and history; (2) by placing him in relation with his physical environment by means of the so-called nature studies—physics, biology, chemistry, etc.; (3) by bringing him into relation with his social environment by means of sociological and political studies. Such an ideal, worked out under the conditions outlined, should result in a youth who possesses at once a sound body, adaptability, clear judgment, and individuality.

With this analysis in mind, a careful study of the selections from the Essays must convince one that, in his educational views, Montaigne was not only far in advance of his own age, but, in some respects, of the present time as well. By common consent France, Germany, England, and the United States lead the world in matters educational. France trains to make soldiers and artisans. The Lehrplan of 1892 shows that Germany's efforts are directed toward the training of soldiers and patriots. England, until the last half century, made no provision for popular education. Even at the present time her educational system, like that of the United States, has for its unconscious purpose the preservation of society under democratic institutions, and fails to show a clear recognition of the fact that, while education is of fundamental concern in a democracy, it means more than simply a solution of the political problem: it means the solution of the human problem, success in dealing with one's self and one's fellows—Montaigne's ideal and that of all thoughtful educators.

Respect the teacher as we may, we must still admit that the fitting process, no less than the occupation itself, is in most instances narrowing. Name over ten great men, and note how few of the number are the product of the schools. Their education has been general rather than special, vital not technical; one got from actual contact with the actual present, and essentially individualistic. Of all writers, Montaigne realizes this most clearly, and for this reason, I believe, he will be understood and appreciated in the future as he has not been in the past. The history of education in some respects runs parallel to that of religious thought. Churchmen have always resisted all attempts at readjustment, all efforts to suit truth to the time and its needs. Similarly, the history of education is a history of systems based upon ideals rooted entirely in the past, and imposed upon childhood without regard either to its present needs or to its future possibilities. Education, like government, must be a "continuous experiment." A system always assumes certain fixed conditions. Life is vibrant, fluctuant; nothing in it is fixed save the individual human soul, nothing certain save the development of that soul.

Matthew Arnold has given us credit for having solved the political problem, and in moments of self-congratulation we indulge the thought that we have the answer to all questions, forgetful that inflexibility, against which Montaigne hurls some of his heaviest denunciations, is not the exclusive characteristic of a monarchy. We dimly perceive a "lock-step in education," but fail to relate it in any way to the creed, "All men are born free and equal." Dogma is dogma, whether emanating from the

Declaration of Independence or from a great church. A democracy may lacerate and crush, though we hypnotize ourselves to believe the contrary. Our own age, too, presents a panacea for the ills of mankind—the adjustment of the relations of capital and labour. So did the sixteenth century think to change men's nature with a new religion, and the seventeenth and eighteenth centuries sought the same end by granting freedom in politics. Humanity is too complex to reach the millennium through any single revolution, whether it be in religion, politics, or education. Montaigne saw this vaguely, yet more clearly than did Rousseau two hundred years later, or than many of us in the United States in the year of our Lord 1898 see it.

Again Montaigne's modernity is shown by his attempt to degrade mere learning from the first place, and to place the emphasis upon fitness for practical life, upon ability to use one's judgment, and upon morality and virtue. He would have large use made of the motor side of humanity—in the language of our decade, "Learn to do by doing"—as is shown by his advocacy of educational games. Things should come before words, through using the senses or by direct experience. In this connection is travel of the greatest importance, especially in acquiring modern languages, which should come first in the course, Latin and Greek last. History is to be taught with the Herbartian aim in view, and co-ordination is foreshadowed.

Our present growing custom of decorating schoolrooms was anticipated by Montaigne in order that "where children find their duty, there they may also find their pleasure." The teacher is the school, therefore exercise the greatest care in choosing the person to whom you intrust your child. While the complete liberation of the human spirit can be effected only through self-activity ranging over the whole field of human inquiry, that knowledge is of most worth that stands in the closest relation to the highest needs of man; that will minister not only to the largest personal growth, but to the duties and privileges incumbent upon him as a citizen of the state; that will satisfy a child's insistent needs and, at the same time, fit him for the life in which he is to play a part. Methods must be varied, new methods devised to suit new ideals, and instruction purely *livresque* avoided. The child himself must be studied to determine "what his childish prognostics indicate," and his sound mind assisted by a sound body.

But most of all are we to reverence the individual, break down every barrier, and bring into activity that precious gift which sees, feels, creates. Montaigne never loses sight of the transcendent value of the individual human soul. This is the meaning of what, for want of insight, has been called his egotism. If there be one ideal which more than any other fills the heart of those who are striving to solve the educational problem, and through it the human problem, it is the right unfolding of the individual human spirit. A feeling is abroad that possibly in our endeavour to educate *every* one, we have neglected or crushed every *one*. In the face of such an accusation, it is most inspiring to come upon this message from a man of insight and broad vision; one who knew all the past, but fixed his eyes steadily upon the present; a man who lived completely in the spirit of his own time, but unwarped by the exigencies of any vocation. Educate not men only, but a man; educate him not by pouring in, nor even by drawing out; surround him with conditions favourable to growth, the unfolding of a complete man—a strong, self-reliant, and self-directing individuality.

Montaigne, Locke, and Rousseau.

A prominent American educator has remarked that the ideas which we attribute to Montaigne are hundreds and thousands of years old. "The Book of the Dead, the Talmud, the writings of the Persians and Hindoos, the books and classics of the Chinese, to say nothing of the educational writings of Plato, Aristotle, Quintilian, and others, contain vast stores from which Rabelais, Montaigne, Mulcaster, Comenius, Rousseau, and all the others have drawn." To this we may say that Montaigne would be the first to disclaim originality, for "Truth and reason are common to all, and belong no more to him who spoke them first than to him who shall speak them hereafter." At the same time, it must be admitted that the ideas of the ancients are found simply as detached statements. Montaigne was the first thinker to develop the truths bequeathed by the ages into a connected, though not formal system of education, and to show their relation to himself as an individual and to his own time. Later writers drew upon him rather than upon his predecessors. Coste was the first to point out Locke's debt to Montaigne, and Mr. Quick admits that " the chief importance of the Thoughts is due to the prominence given by Locke to truths which had already been set forth by Montaigne." "This fine writer, with his clearness of thought and expression, set himself against bookishness, and so became the great spokesman of those who were dissatisfied with the school system of the Renaissance."

The table given below will illustrate the close dependence of Locke and Rousseau upon Montaigne. The verbal similarity is the more striking when we remember that Montaigne wrote in sixteenth century French, Locke in seventeenth century English, and Rousseau in eighteenth century French. Besides the agreement shown, it should be observed that all three lay stress upon private instruction—the care of the single child—which is not remarkable when we remember the character of the schools of their respective times. All insist, too, upon the vernacular first, modern languages next, then Latin and Greek—a plan followed by Ratich and Comenius. In this connection I wish, also, to direct the attention of the German reader to Dr. F. A. Arnstädt's valuable François Rabelais und sein Traité D'Education mit besonderer Berücksichtigung der pädagogischen Grundsätze Montaigne's, Locke's, und Rousseau's (Leipzig, 1872).

Choice of Tutor.

MONTAIGNE.
Upon the choice of the tutor you shall provide for your son depends the whole success of his education. . . . I would rather commend a tutor for having a well-made than a well-filled head, yet both are desirable. (Pp. 27, 28.)

LOCKE.
In the whole Business of Education there is nothing like to be less harken'd to, or harder to be well observ'd than . . . the getting of a Tutor. (Sec. 90.)
The Reputation of a sober Man with a good Stock of Learning (which is all usually required in a Tutor) will not be enough to serve your Turn. (Sec. 92.) Locke: Some Thoughts concerning Education. Quick, London, 1892.

ROUSSEAU.
A teacher! what an exalted soul he should be! (P. 16.) Is it impossible to find this rare mortal? But suppose we have found this prodigy? It is by considering what he ought to do that we shall see what he ought to be. (P. 17.) Rousseau, Émile. Payne, New York, 1893.

Use of Motor Side in Educational Games.

MONTAIGNE.
My father proposed to teach me Greek by a new device, making of it a sort of sport and recreation. We tossed declensions and conjugations to and fro, after the manner of those who by certain games at table and chess learn geometry and arithmetic. (P. 79.)

LOCKE.
Make what you would have them do a Recreation to them and not a Business. (Sec. 129.)
Children may be *taught to read*, without perceiving it to be anything but a Sport. (Sec. 149.)

ROUSSEAU.
His sports are his occupations, and he feels no difference between them. (P. 127.)
You may see him doing the most serious things under the guise of play. (P. 128.)

See also Fénelon, Comenius, Pestalozzi, Froebel, Richter for the same thought expressed in almost the same language.

Importance of Physical Training.

Montaigne.	Locke.	Rousseau.
It is not enough to fortify his soul, you must also make his muscles strong. (P. 36.) Accustom the child to heat and cold, wind and sun, and to dangers that he ought to despise. (P. 62.)	A Sound Mind in a sound Body is a short but full Description of a happy State in this World. (Sec. 1.) He will accustom himself to Heat and Cold, Shine and Rain; all which, if a Man's Body will not endure, it will serve him to very little purpose in this World. (Sec. 9.)	We may make a man robust without endangering his health. . . . Harden their bodies to the changes of seasons, climates, and elements, as well as to hunger, thirst, and fatigue. (P. 13.)

Condemn Harsh Methods. School Life should be made Pleasant.

Montaigne.	Locke.	Rousseau.
Away with this violence! Away with this compulsion! Nothing, I believe, more dulls and degenerates a well-born nature. (P. 61.) Were it left to my ordering, I would paint the school with pictures of Joy and Gladness, Flora and the Graces. . . . Where their profit is, there should also be their pleasure. (Pp. 62, 63.)	Great severity of Punishment does but very little Good, nay great Harm in Education: and I believe it will be found *cæteris paribus* those Children who have been most chastis'd seldom make the best men. (Sec. 43.) Give them a Liking and Inclination to what you propose to them to be learn'd. (Sec. 72.)	The age of mirth is passed in the midst of tears, chastisements, threats, and slavery . . . without any assurance that such sacrifices will ever be useful. . . . Love childhood; encourage its sports, its pleasures, its amiable instincts. (P. 45.)

See also Comenius, Ratich, Fénelon, Basedow, Pestalozzi, Froebel.

Train for Practical Life.

MONTAIGNE.	LOCKE.	ROUSSEAU.
Let us make choice of those studies which directly and professedly serve to the instruction and use of life ... and even in those things that are useful, there are many points it would be better to leave alone, and, following Socrates' direction, limit our studies to those of real utility. (Pp. 48, 49.)	And since it can not be hop'd he should have Time and Strength to learn all things, most Pains should be taken about that which is most necessary; and that principally look'd after which will be of most and frequentest Use to him in the World. (Sec. 94.)	When one has been taught as his most important lesson to desire nothing in the way of knowledge, save what is useful, he asks questions like Socrates. (P. 156.) Let us always recollect that there is no honour without utility. (P. 180.)

Importance of History.

MONTAIGNE.	LOCKE.	ROUSSEAU.
History is my chief study. (P. 20.) It is of inestimable value to such as can make use of it. (P. 42.)	I recommend it ... as one of the most useful studies, he can apply himself to. (Of Study.)	It is through this study he will read hearts without philosophic lectures, and without the risk of spoiling his own. (P. 213.)

Character most Important.

MONTAIGNE.	LOCKE.	ROUSSEAU.
All other learning is hurtful to him who has not the knowledge of honesty and goodness. (P. 102.)	Learning must be had, but in the second Place as subservient only to greater Qualities. (Sec. 147.)	I would make it seem that *justice* and *goodness* are not merely abstract terms, pure moral creations formed by the understanding, but real affections of the soul enlightened by reason. (P. 210.)

See also Fénelon, Pestalozzi, Froebel, Comenius.

Some Modern Educational Ideas anticipated by Montaigne.

1. "The teacher is the school." Pp. 27, 28.
2. "Learn to do by doing." Pp. 66, 67, 79, 104–106.
3. Great importance of physical training. Pp. 35, 36, 37, 61, 62.
4. Make school life and school surroundings pleasant. Pp. 61–63, 85.
5. Harsh methods do not produce the best results. Pp. 61, 62, 116, 136.
6. Train for practical life. Pp. 48–50, 57, 92, 96, 100, 101, 106, 107.
7. Importance of History as a culture study. Pp. 42, 43, 46, 57, 147.
8. Apperception and co-ordination foreshadowed. Pp. 29, 30, 95, 96.
9. Child study suggested. Pp. 28, 29, 56.
10. Mere memorizing disparaged. Pp. 28, 29, 30, 33, 34, 42, 139.
11. Train the child's judgment. Pp. 31, 95, 99, 105, 106.
12. Travel of great importance. Pp. 34, 35, 44, 46.
13. Inculcate patriotism. Pp. 39, 40.
14. Too much book study harmful. Pp. 33, 58, 59, 67, 68, 96–98, 108, 109, 131–133, 139, 140.
15. "Things before words." Pp. 44, 68–72.
16. Early reading should be entertaining. Pp. 81, 82.
17. Make use of play instinct. Pp. 79, 125, 126.
18. Train the whole man. Pp. 60, 61.
19. Character all important. Pp. 50, 54, 66, 92, 103, 127, 128.
20. Consult the individual. Pp. 25, 29, 56, 128.
21. Not pouring in nor drawing out, but growth. Pp. 24, 25, 33, 34, 48, 49, 66, 67.

OF THE EDUCATION OF CHILDREN.

To MADAME DIANE DE FOIX, COUNTESS OF GURSON.

Book I, Chapter XXV.

I HAVE never known a father, no matter how crooked and deformed his son might be,

Montaigne's intellectual limitations.

who would either altogether cast him off, or refuse to acknowledge him as his own. And yet, unless totally blinded in his affection, he plainly perceived the defects in the son, who nevertheless was his own. So it is with myself. I see better than any one else that what I have set down is nothing but the fond imaginations of a man who, in his youth, has tasted nothing but the crust, and has retained nothing but a general and unformed impression; a little of everything, and nothing to the purpose, after the French manner. To be sure, I know there is a science of medicine, a course of law, four parts of mathematics, and I have a general idea what all these are about. I also know that knowledge in general tends to the service of life. But to wade further, to plod upon Aristotle, the monarch of our modern doctrines, to continue obstinately any one study, I confess I never did it, nor is there a single art of which I know so much as the rudiments. There is no scholar, be he of the lowest class, who may not consider himself wiser than I, for I should not be able to examine him in his first lesson. If forced to it I should be obliged, in my own defense, to ask him some general question to try his natural judgment; something as strange and unknown to him as his lesson is to me. I have never seriously read books of solid learning except Plutarch and Seneca, from whom, as the Danaides, I draw my water, incessantly filling and as fast emptying. Some things I fasten to this paper, but to myself nothing at all.

History is my chief study, and I am also particularly fond of poetry. Cleanthes remarked that the voice being forcibly pent up in a narrow passage of a trumpet at last issues forth stronger and more shrill. So it seems to me, that a sentence couched in the harmony of verse darts out more briskly upon the understanding, and strikes[1] both ear and apprehension with more pleasure. Concerning my natural faculties, of which you behold an example, I perceive them to be indifferent. My fancy

and my judgment march in an uncertain way—
as it were, groping, staggering, and stumbling.
And when I have gone as far as I can I have
in no way satisfied myself. The farther I sail
the more land I descry, and that so dimmed
with fogs and overcast with clouds my sight
is weakened. And then, undertaking to speak
of all that presents itself to my mind, it happens I come upon in good authors these very
subjects I have contemplated treating, as just
now I did while reading Plutarch's Discourse
on the Power of Imagination. In comparison
with these great men I acknowledge myself so
poor, so weak, so dull and flat, that I am forced
both to pity and despise myself. And yet I
am pleased that my opinions have often the grace to coincide with theirs, and that I can follow them,

His opinions coincide with those of other writers.

though from afar, and can say, "Ah, that is so."
I possess that which many other men have not—
the ability to see there is the greatest difference
between these wise men and myself; nevertheless I suffer my inventions to run along, weak
and faint though they are, without bungling
or mending the faults which the comparison
has shown me. A man needs a strong back
to keep pace with these men. The indiscreet
scribblers of our age, who, throughout their

4

trivial compositions, insert whole sentences from ancient authors, supposing by such filching to purchase honour and reputation for themselves, do quite the contrary. The comparison renders the appearance of their own writings so pale and sallow that they lose much more than they gain.

The philosophers Chrysippus and Epicurus were in this matter quite contrary. The first was accustomed to bring in among his writings not only whole sentences, but whole books, of other authors—in one instance the whole Medea of Euripides. Apollodorus[2] was wont to say of him that, if one should take from his books all he had stolen from others, he would leave nothing but blank paper. On the other hand, Epicurus,[3] in the three hundred volumes he left behind him, did not make use of so much as one quotation.

<small>Chrysippus and Epicurus compared.</small>

The other day I had this experience. I was reading a book, and after I had run dreaming over a great many words so dull, so insipid, so devoid of all wit and common sense that they were really only French words, I came at last to something that was lofty and rich and elevated to the very clouds. Had the declivity

<small>Quotations often bring out an author's weakness.</small>

been easy or the ascent gradual there had been some excuse, but it was so perpendicular a precipice, and so wholly cut off from the rest of the work, that at the first six words I found myself flying into the other world, and discovered the valley whence I came so deep and low that I have not had the heart to descend into it again. If I should fill one of my discourses with such rich spoils as these, it would but too truly manifest the imperfection of my own writing. To reprove my own faults in others seems to me no more unreasonable than to condemn, as I often do, those of others in myself. I know how over-boldly, at all times, I try to equal my filchings, and to march hand in hand with them; not without the fond hope that I may perhaps be able to blear the eyes of my judges from discerning the difference. . . . Yet I never quote others but that I may the better express myself. . . . I aim at nothing but to reveal myself, and if, in the meantime, a new book or friend change me, I will be some one else to-morrow.⁴ However, these are but my humours and opinions, and I speak them to show what my idea is, and not what ought to be believed. I have no authority to purchase belief, neither do I desire it, knowing well that I am not sufficiently taught to instruct others.

A friend of mine, having read the preceding chapter, told me, the other day, in my own house, I should have enlarged a little more upon the education of children.* Now, madam, were my abilities equal to the subject, I could not possibly employ them better than in presenting them to your little son. Moreover, the old right you have ever had and still have over my service urges me with more than ordinary respect to wish all honour, welfare, and advantage to whatever may in any way concern you and yours. I mean to show by this that the greatest and most important difficulty of human effort is the training and education of children.⁵

<small>Montaigne introduces his subject of education.</small>

In matters of husbandry, all that precedes sowing, setting, and planting, even planting itself, is certain and easy. But when that which was sown, set, and planted takes life, there is a great deal more to be done, and it requires great care to bring it to perfection. So with men, continual cares, diligent attendance, doubts and fears, daily wait upon their parents and tutors before they can be nurtured

<small>Relation of children's early inclinations to their education.</small>

---

* Cotton interpolates: "Which how fit I am to do let my friends flatter me if they please. I have in the meantime no such opinion of my own talent as to promise myself any very good success from my endeavour."

and brought to any good.⁶ Their inclinations, while they are young, are so uncertain, their dispositions so variable, their promises so changing, their hopes so false, and their actions so doubtful, that it is very hard, even for the wisest, to place any certain judgment upon them or to feel assured of success. Look at Cymon and Themistocles, and a thousand others, whose manhood gave the lie to the ill-promise of their early youth. The young whelps of both dogs and bears show their natural disposition from the first; but men embracing this custom or fashion, following that humour or opinion, admitting this or that passion, conforming to certain laws, are changed and soon disguised. And yet, for want of a ready foresight of the natural propensity of the mind, much time is wasted in trying to teach children those things for which, by their natural constitution, they are totally unfit. Notwithstanding these difficulties my advice is, to bring them up in the best and most profitable studies without being too superstitious or taking too much notice of those light prognostics which they give of themselves in their infancy. Without offence to Plato, in his Republic, I think he allows them too much authority.⁷

Madam, learning joined with true knowledge is an especial and graceful ornament, and an implement of wonderful use and consequence, particularly to persons raised to that degree of fortune in which you are placed. And truly, learning has not her true form, nor can she show her beautiful lineaments, if she fall into the hands of base and vile persons. Famous Torquato Tasso says: "Philosophy is a rich and noble queen, and, knowing her own worth, graciously smiles upon and lovingly embraces princes and noblemen, if they become suitors to her, admitting them as her minions and gently affording them all the favours she can. On the other hand, if she be wooed by clowns and such base people, she considers herself disparaged and disgraced, having nothing in common with them." We know by experience that if a true gentleman or nobleman follows philosophy with any attention, he will learn and know more of her and make a better scholar in one year than a base fellow will in seven, though he pursue her never so attentively. She is much more ready to assist in the conduct of war, in the government of a people, in negotiating peace with a foreign prince, than she is to form a syllogism in logic,

Education of especial value to those of noble birth.

to plead a cause at the bar, or to prescribe a dose of pills. So, noble lady, I can not persuade myself that you will either forget or neglect this point concerning the education of your children, since you have tasted the delights of learning and are descended from so noble a race. We still possess the learned compositions of the ancient and noble Counts of Foix, from whom both you and your husband are descended, and of Francis, Lord of Candale, your worthy uncle, who daily shows forth the matchless quality of a house which will extend itself to many ages. I shall therefore make you acquainted with an idea of mine, which I hold, contrary to the common usage.

Upon the choice of a tutor you shall provide for your son depends the whole success of his education and bringing up. A gentleman born of noble parentage and heir of a house which aims at true learning should be disciplined not so much for the practical use he could make of it—so abject an end is unworthy the grace and favour of the Muses, and, besides, bids for the regard of others—not for external use and ornament, but to adorn and enrich his inward mind, desiring rather to form an able and efficient man than a learned man. My desire is, therefore,

Choice of tutor all-important.

that the parents or guardians of such a gentleman be very careful in choosing his tutor, whom I would commend for having a well-made[8] rather than a well-filled head, yet both are desirable. And I would prefer wisdom, judgment, civil manners, and modest behaviour to bare and mere literal learning. And in his teaching I would advise a new course. Some never cease brawling in their pupils' ears, as if they were pouring into a funnel, to follow their book. I would have a tutor correct this, and on taking up a subject, according to the child's capacity, I would have him show it to his pupil, who may know thereby a little of all things, and how to choose and distinguish them without the help of others; sometimes opening for him the way, at other times leaving him to open it for himself. I would not have the tutor do all the talking, but allow the pupil to speak when his turn comes. Socrates, and after him Arcesilaus, made their pupils speak first, and then would speak themselves. "Obest plerumque iis, qui discere volunt auctoritas eorum qui docent."[9] ("Most commonly the authority of those who teach hinders those who would learn.") The tutor should make his pupil, like a young horse, trot before him in order that he may the better judge of his pace, determine how long he will hold out, and, accordingly, what may fit his strength. Lacking this knowledge we often spoil all. To make a good choice and to keep the right proportions is one of the hardest things I know. It is a sign of a noble and undaunted spirit, to know how far to condescend to childish proceedings, how to second, and how to guide them. As for myself, I can more easily walk up than down a hill.

Child study.

Those who, according to our way of teaching, undertake in the same lessons and in the same manner of instruction to direct many pupils of different intellects and dispositions, seldom meet with more than two or three who reap any good by their discipline or who come to any perfection.

Individual teaching favoured.

I would not only have the instructor demand an account of the words contained in a lesson, but of the sense and substance; and judge of the profit he has made of it, not by the testimony of his memory but by his own judgment. What he has lately learned cause him to set forth in a hundred various ways, and then to apply it to as many different subjects as possible, to determine whether he has apprehended the same and

Apperception and co-ordination.

made it a part of himself,[10] taking instruction of his progress from the Institutions of Plato. It is a sign of crudity and indigestion for a man to throw up his meat as he swallowed it. The stomach has not done its work unless it has changed the form and altered the condition of the food given to it. We see men gape after nothing but learning, and when they say such a one is a learned man, they think they have said enough. Our minds move at another's pleasure, bound and compelled to serve the fancies of others, brought under by authority and forced to accept their bare lesson. We have been so subjected to harp upon one string, that we have no power left to carry out our own wills. Our vigour and liberty are extinct. "Nunquam tutelæ suæ fiunt."[11] ("They never become their own masters.")

Dogmatism illustrated. It was my fortune to become acquainted with an honest man at Pisa, but such an Aristotelian as to hold this unalterable position: "That a conformity to Aristotle's doctrine was the true touchstone of all solid thinking and perfect truth; for whatever did not conform to it was but fond chimeras and idle humours, inasmuch as he had known all, seen all, and said all." This proposition of his, being somewhat maliciously inter-

OF THE EDUCATION OF CHILDREN. 31

preted by others a long time after, brought him in great danger of the inquisition of Rome.

I would have the tutor make the child examine and thoroughly sift all things, and harbour nothing in his head by mere authority or upon trust. Aristotle's principles should no more be axioms to him than those of the Stoics or Epicureans. Let different judgments be submitted to him; he may be able to distinguish truth from falsehood; if not, he may remain in doubt.

Pupil's own judgment should be cultivated.

> "No less it pleases me
> To doubt, than wise to be." [12]

If by his own thinking he embraces the opinions of Xenophon or of Plato, the opinions will be no longer theirs, but will become his own. He that merely follows another, seeks nothing, finds nothing. "Non sumus sub rege; sibi quisque se vindicet." [13] ("We are not under a king; each one may dispose of himself.") Let him at least know that he does know. He must imbibe their knowledge, but not adopt their dogmas; when he knows how to apply, he may at once forget when or whence he had his learning.

Truth and reason are common to all, and belong no more to him who spoke them first than to him who shall speak them hereafter. It is no more according to Plato's opinion than to mine, since both he and I under- stand and see alike. Bees here and there suck this and cull that flower, but afterward they produce the honey which is peculiarly their own, and is no longer thyme or marjoram. So of matter borrowed of others, one may lawfully alter, transform, and blend it to compile a perfect piece of work altogether his own; always provided his judgment, his work, and study tend to nothing but to make the same perfect. Let him thoroughly conceal whence he had any help, and make no show of anything but of what he has made himself. Pirates, pilferers, and borrowers make a show of their purchases and buildings, but do not tell how they come by the money. You do not see the secret fees or bribes lawyers take of their clients, but you are sure to discover the cases they win, the homes they provide for their children, the fine houses they build. No man makes a show of his revenue, or at least of how he gets it, but every one of his purchases.

[margin: Borrowed matter to be assimilated.]

Study should make us wiser. It is the understanding, says Epicharmus, that sees and hears, that moves, sways, and rules all. Everything else is blind, senseless, and without spirit, and by depriving a pupil of liberty to do things for himself we make him servile and cowardly. Who ever inquires of his pupil what he thinks of rhetoric, of grammar, of this or of that sentence of Cicero? Our teachers stick them full-feathered in our memories, and there establish them like oracles, of which the very words and letters are the substance of the thing."[14] To know by heart only is not to know at all; it is simply to keep what one has committed to his memory. What a man knows directly, that will he dispose of without turning to his book or looking to his pattern. A mere bookish knowledge is useless. It may embellish actions, but it is not a foundation for them. According to Plato, constancy, faith, and sincerity are true philosophy. As for other kinds of knowledge, they are garish paintings. Le Paluel and Pompey, those two noted dancers of our time, might as well teach a man to do their tricks and high capers by simply looking on and without stirring out of his place, as for some pedantical fellow to instruct our mind without moving or putting it to work. I should like to find one who would teach us to manage a horse, to toss a spear, to shoot, to

Apperception, not mere memorizing.

play upon the lute, or to sing without any practice; yet these men would teach us to judge and how to speak well without any exercise in speaking or judging. Now, while we are in our apprenticeship to learning, actions or objects which present themselves to our eyes may serve us instead of a book. The knavish trick of a page, the foolishness of a servant, a jest at table, are so many new subjects for us to work upon.

And for this very reason the society of men, the visiting of foreign countries, observing people and strange customs, are very necessary; not to be able, after the manner of our young French gallants, to repeat how many paces the Santa Rotunda [15] is in circuit, or of the richness of Signiora Livia's attire, or how much longer or broader the face of Nero is, which they have seen in some old ruin of Italy, than one seen on some medal. But they should be able to give an account of the ideas, manners, customs, and laws of the nations they have visited. That he may whet and sharpen his wits by rubbing them upon those of others, I would have a boy sent abroad very young; and in order to kill two birds with one stone, he should first see those neighbouring countries whose languages

Travel of great importance.

OF THE EDUCATION OF CHILDREN. 35

differ most from ours. For unless a man's tongue be formed to them in his youth, he can never acquire the true pronunciation.

We see it received as a common opinion of the wiser sort, that a child should not be dandled and brought up in his mother's lap.¹⁶ Their natural affection is apt to make the most discreet of parents so overfond that they can not find it in their hearts to see their children checked, corrected, or chastised. Neither will parents allow them to be brought up in hardships and deprivations, as they ought to be. It would grieve them to see their children come home from manly exercise sweaty and dusty, to drink cold water when they are hot, to mount an unruly horse, or to take a foil in hand against a skilful fencer, or so much as to shoot off an arquebuse. And yet there is no other way. Whoever would have a boy good for anything when he becomes a man, must not spare him when young, and must very often transgress the rules of medicine.

Parents should not spoil their children.

> "Vitamque sub divo et trepidis agat
> In rebus." ¹⁷

("He must sharp cold and scorching heat despise,
And most tempt danger where most danger lies.")

It is not enough to fortify his soul; you must also make his muscles strong. The mind **Importance of physical training.** will be oppressed if not assisted by the body; it is too much for her alone to discharge two offices. I know very well how mine groans under a tender and delicate body that eternally leans and presses upon it. In my reading I often perceive how authors sometimes commend persons for magnanimity and fortitude which really proceed from a thick skin and hard bones. I have known men, women, and children possessing so hard and so insensible a body that a blow with a cudgel would hurt them less than a flip of a finger would me, and who would neither cry out nor wince, beat them all you would. When wrestlers counterfeit the patience of philosophers, they show the strength of their muscles rather than stoutness of heart. Now, to be inured to labour is to be able to bear pain. "Labor callum obducit dolori."[18] ("Labor hardens us against pain.")

A boy must be broken in by the hardship of severe exercises to endure the pain of colic, of cauteries, of falls, of dislocations, and even of imprisonment and the rack itself.[19] By misfortune he may be reduced to the worst of these, which, as we have seen, sometimes befall the good as well as the bad. As for proofs, in our present civil war whoever draws his sword against the laws, threatens all honest men with the whip and halter.

Moreover, by living at home the authority of the tutor, which ought to be sovereign over the child, is often checked, interrupted, and hindered by the presence of the parents. Besides, the respect the whole household bear him as their master's son is, in my opinion, no small hindrance during these tender years.

Home influences often interfere with the child's training.

In my intercourse with men of the world I have often observed this fault, that, instead of gathering information from others, we make it our whole business to give them our own, and are more concerned how to expose and set out our own commodities than how to acquire new. Silence and modesty are excellent qualities in conversation, and one should therefore train up the boy to be sparing and close-handed with what he knows when once acquired, and to refrain from reproving every idle saying or ridiculous story spoken or told in his presence.[20] It is a great rudeness to controvert everything that is not agreeable to our palate. Let him be

Children should be seen, not heard.

satisfied with correcting himself, and not seem to condemn in others what he would not do himself, nor dispute against common custom. "Licet sapere, sine pompa, sine invidia."[21] ("Let him be wise without ostentation and without envy.") Let him avoid those ancient fashions and the childish ambition of trying to appear something better and greater than other people, proving himself in reality something less; and, as though finding fault were a proof of genius, seeking to found a special reputation thereon. It becomes none but great poets to make use of poetic license, so it is intolerable that any but men of great and illustrious souls should be privileged above the authority of custom. "Si quid Socrates et Aristippus contra morem et consuetudinem fecerunt; idem sibi ne arbitretur licere; magis enim illi et divinis bonis hanc licentiam assequebantur."[22] ("If Socrates and Aristippus have transgressed the rules of custom, let him not think he is licensed to do the same, for it was by great and sovereign virtues they obtained this privilege.")

Only great minds should assume unusual privileges.

The boy should be instructed not to engage in dispute except with a champion worthy of him and even then not to make use of all

OF THE EDUCATION OF CHILDREN. 39

the little subtleties that seem suited to his purpose, but only of such as may best serve him on that occasion. Let him be taught to be nice in his choice of reasons, to be sure they are pertinent, and to study brevity. Above all, let him acquiesce and submit to truth as soon as he shall discover it, whether in his opponent's argument or upon better consideration of his own. He will never be raised to any position above others for a mere clatter of words and syllogisms. Nor shall he bind himself to defend a cause further than he may approve of it, nor engage in that trade when the liberty of recantation and getting off upon better thoughts are to be sold for ready money. "Neque, ut omnia quæ præscripta et imperata sint defendat, necessitate ulla cogitur."[23] ("Neither is there any necessity or obligation upon him at all that he should defend all things that are recommended and commanded him.")

<small>Train pupils to be fair in argument.</small>

If the tutor be of my humour, he will teach his pupil to be a good and loyal subject to his prince, and a most affectionate and courageous gentleman in all that may concern the honour of his sovereign and the good of his country, and endeavour to

<small>Patriotism inculcated.</small>

suppress in him the desire of having any other tie to his king's service than public duty. Such bonds are inconsistent with the liberty every honest man should possess. A man's judgment is bribed by particular favours and obligations, and is either blinded and less free to exercise its functions or is blemished with ingratitude. A man purely a courtier has neither power nor wit to speak or to think otherwise than favourably of his master, who among so many thousand subjects has made choice of him alone. This favour and the profit flowing from it must needs—and not without some show of reason—corrupt his freedom and dazzle his judgment. The language of courtiers differs from that of other men, and in consequence they are not accepted as judges in these matters.

Let conscience and virtue shine in his speech, and let him have reason for his chief guide. Make him understand that to acknowledge the error he shall discover in his own argument, though only perceived by himself, is an effect of judgment and sincerity, which are the principal things he is to seek after; that obstinacy and contention are common qualities best becoming a mean soul; and that to recollect and to correct himself and to forsake a bad

Errors should be frankly acknowledged.

argument in the heat of dispute are noble and rare philosophic qualities.

In company he should have his eye and ear in every corner of the room, for I notice that the places of greatest honour are usually taken by the most unworthy and least capable, and that the greatest fortunes are not always possessed by the best men. I have been present when those at the upper end of the table have been only commending the hangings about the room or the flavour of the wine, while at the lower end many fine things have been lost or thrown away. Let him examine every one's talent— that of a herdsman, a mason, a stranger, or a traveller. A man may learn something from every one of these which he can use at some time or another. Even the folly and weakness of others will contribute to his instruction. By observing the graces and manners of others, he will acquire for himself the emulation of the good and a contempt for the bad. Let an honest curiosity be awakened in him to search out the nature and design of all things. Let him investigate whatever is singular and rare about him— a fine building, a fountain, an eminent man, the place where a battle was anciently fought, the passage of Cæsar or of Charlemagne.

General observation of great value.

"Quæ tellus sit lenta gelu, quæ putris ab æstu,
Ventus in Italiam qui bene vela ferat."[24]

("What lands are frozen, what are parched explore,
And what wind bears us to the Italian shore.")

Let him inquire into the manners, revenues, and alliances of princes, things in themselves very pleasant to learn and very useful to know. In this acquaintance of men, my purpose is that he should give his chief attention to those who live in the records of history.

Scope of history. He shall by the aid of books inform himself of the worthiest minds of the best ages. History is an idle study to those who choose to make it so, but of inestimable value to such as can make use of it; the only study, Plato says, the Lacedæmonians reserved to themselves. Touching this point, what profit may he not reap by reading the Lives of Plutarch?[25] But, above all, let the tutor remember to what end his instruction is directed, and not so much imprint in his pupil's memory the date of the ruin of Carthage as the character of Hannibal and of Scipio; nor so much where Marcellus died as why it was unworthy of his duty that he died there. Let him read history, not as an amusing narrative, but as a discipline of the judgment. It is this study to which, in my opinion, we apply ourselves with the most differing and uncertain measures. I have read a hundred things in Livy that another has not, or has not taken the least notice of; and Plutarch has read a hundred more than ever I could find, or than, peradventure, the author ever set down. To some it is a mere language study, but to others a perfect anatomy of philosophy, by which the most secret and abstruse parts of our human natures are penetrated. There are in Plutarch many discourses worthy of being carefully read and observed, for he is, in my opinion, the greatest master in that kind of writing; but there are a thousand other matters which he has only touched upon, where he only points with his finger to direct us which way we may go if we will. He contents himself sometimes with only giving one brief touch to the main point of the question, and leaves the rest for us to find out for ourselves. For example, he says: "The inhabitants of Asia come to be vassals of one only, not being able to pronounce the syllable No."[26] This saying of his gave perhaps both subject and occasion to my friend La Boëtie[27] to write his Voluntary Servitude. To Plutarch, a slight action in a man's life or a word that seems of little importance to others will serve for a whole discourse. It is a pity men of understanding should so often affect brevity; no doubt their reputation is the better for it, but we the worse. Plutarch would rather have us applaud his judgment than commend his knowledge, and would rather leave us with an appetite for more, than glutted with what we have already read. He knew very well that a man may say too much upon even the best subjects, and that Alexandrides did justly reprove him who made very elegant but long speeches. "O stranger," he said, "you speak what you should, but not in the way you should."[28] Such as have lean bodies stuff themselves out with clothes; so they who are defective in matter endeavour to make amends with words.

Human understanding is marvellously enlightened by daily conversation with men and by travelling abroad. In ourselves we are dull and stupid, and have our sight limited to the end of our nose. When Socrates was asked of what country he was, he did not answer, "Of Athens," but "Of the world."[29] His imagination was rich and expansive, and he embraced the whole world for his country, extending his society, his friendship, his knowledge to all mankind, not as we do, who look no farther than our feet. When the vines of our village are nipped by frost,

Broadening influence of travel.

the parish priest immediately concludes that the wrath of God hangs over our head and threatens all mankind, and says that the cannibals have already got the pip. Who is it, seeing these civil wars of ours, does not cry out that the machine of the world is upsetting and that the day of judgment is at hand, never remembering that there have been many worse revolutions, and that in the meantime people are very happy in ten thousand other parts of the earth and never think of us. For my part, considering the license that always attends such commotions, I wonder they are so moderate and that there is no more mischief done. He who feels the hailstones upon his head thinks the whole hemisphere to be in storm and tempest; like the ridiculous Savoyard, who said very gravely "that if the King of France had managed well he might in time have come to be the steward in the household of the duke his master." In his shallow imagination he could not conceive how any one could be greater than the Duke of Savoy. In truth, we are all addicted to this error, an error of very pernicious consequence. But whoever shall represent to his fancy, as in a picture, that great image of our mother Nature attired in her richest robes, sitting on the throne of her majesty, and in her visage shall read so general and so constant a variety; whoever shall observe himself in that picture, and not himself, but a whole kingdom, no bigger than the least touch of a pencil compared with the whole—that man alone is able to value things according to their true estimate and grandeur.

This great world, which some multiply as several species under one genus, is the true mirror wherein we must look in order to know ourselves as we should. In short, I would have this to be the book my young gentleman should study with most attention. Many strange humours, many sects, many judgments, opinions, laws, and customs, teach us to judge rightly of our own actions, to correct our faults, and to inform our understanding, which is no trivial lesson. So many changes of states and kingdoms, so many falls of princes and revolutions of public opinion, ought to teach us not to wonder at our own. So many great names, so many famous victories and conquests swallowed in oblivion, render ridiculous the hope of immortalizing our names by taking half a score light horse, or a paltry turret which is only known by its fall. The pride and arrogance of so many foreign pomps and ceremonies, the inflated majesty of so many

[sidenote: The world the best text-book.]

OF THE EDUCATION OF CHILDREN. 47

courts, accustom and fortify our sight to behold the lustre of our own without blinking. The many millions of men laid in their graves before us encourage us not to fear or be dismayed to go and meet such good company in the other world.

Pythagoras was wont to say that our life resembles the great and populous assembly of the Olympic games. Some exercise the body for glory, others carry merchandise to sell for profit; there are also some, and not the worst sort either, who seek after no other advantage than to look on and consider how and why everything is done, and to be inactive spectators of the lives and actions of other men, thereby the better to judge of and to regulate their own.[30]

Pythagoras compares life to the Olympic games.

As examples, philosophic discourses may be taken, to which all human action, as to their best rule, ought to be especially directed:

Relation of philosophical examples to life.

"Quid fas optare, quid asper
Utile nummus habet; patriæ carisque propinquis
Quantum clargiri deceat; quem te Deus esse
Jussit, et humana qua parte locatus es in re;
Quid summus, aut quidnam victuri gignimur."[31]

("Think what we are, and for what ends designed;
How we may best through life's long mazes wind;

What we should wish for; how we may discern
The bounds of wealth and its true uses learn;
How fix the portion which we ought to give
To friends, relations, country; how to live
As fits our station; and how best pursue
What God has given us in this world to do.")

In these examples a man shall learn what it is to know, and what it is to be ignorant; what ought to be the end and design of study; what valour, temperance, and justice are; what difference there is between ambition and avarice, bondage and freedom, license and liberty; by what token a man may know true and solid content; to what extent one may fear and apprehend death, pain, or disgrace,

"Et quo quemque modo fugiasque ferasque laborem."[32]
("And what you may avoid, and what must undergo.")

He shall also learn what secret springs move us, and the reason of our various irresolutions; for, I think, the first doctrines with which one seasons his understanding ought to be those that rule his manners and direct his sense; that teach him to know himself, how to live and how to die well. Among the liberal studies let us begin with those which make us free; *Train for practical life.* not that they do not all serve in some measure to the instruction and use of life, as do all other things, but let us make choice of those which directly and professedly serve to that end. If we were once able to restrain the offices of human life within their just and natural limits, we should find that most of the subjects now taught are of no great use to us; and even in those that are useful there are many points it would be better to leave alone, and, following Socrates' direction, limit our studies to those of real utility.

"Sapere aude,
Incipe qui recte vivendi prorogat horam,
Rusticus exspectat, dum defluat amnis; at ille
Labitur et labetur in omne volubilis ævum." [33]

("Dare to be wise, and now begin; the man who has it in his power
To practice virtue, and puts off the hour,
Waits, like a clown, to see the brook run low,
Which onward flows, and will forever flow.")

<small>Useless knowledge.</small> It is mere foolishness to teach our children,

" Quid moveant Pisces, animosaque Signa Leonis,
Lotus et Hesperia quid Capricornus aqua," [34]

(" What influence Pisces and fierce Leo have,
Or Capricornus in the Hesperian wave,")

the knowledge of the stars and the motion of the eighth sphere before their own.

" Τί πλειάδεσσι κάμοί;
Τί δ' ἀστράσιν βοώτεω;" [35]

(" How swift the seven sisters' motions are,
Or the dull churls how slow, what need I care?")

Anaximenes, writing to Pythagoras, said, "To what purpose should I trouble myself in searching out the secrets of the stars, having death or slavery continually before my eyes?"[36] for the kings of Persia were at that time preparing to invade his country. Every one ought to say, "Being assailed, as I am, by ambition, avarice, temerity, and superstition, and having within so many enemies of life, why should I bother my head about the world's revolutions?"

After having taught our pupil what will make him wise and good, you may then teach him the elements of logic, physics, geometry, and rhetoric. After training, he will quickly make his own that science which best pleases him. He should be instructed sometimes by a talk, sometimes by reading. At times the tutor should put the author himself into his hands, at other times give him only the pith and substance of it. And if the tutor does not know enough about books to refer the pupil to the choicest parts, a literary man might be employed to assist in this matter. Who can doubt that this way of teaching is much more easy and natural than that advocated by Gaza,[37] in which the precepts are so intricate and so harsh, and the words so

Method of instruction.

vain, empty, and insignificant, that there is no substance in them, nothing to quicken and elevate the wit and fancy. According to my method of teaching, the mind has something to feed upon and to digest. The fruit, therefore, will not only be much finer, but will also ripen earlier.

It is a thousand pities that matters should be at such a pass, in this age of ours, that philosophy, even with men of understanding, is looked upon as vain and fantastic, a thing of no use, no value, either in opinion or effect. And I think these sophists, by making the study difficult, are to blame for this state of affairs. People do wrong to represent it to children as an extremely difficult task, and set it forth with such a frowning, grim, and formidable aspect. Who has disguised her with this false, pale, and hideous countenance? There is nothing more airy, more gay, more frolicsome. She presents nothing to our eyes and preaches nothing to our ears but feasting and jollity. A sad and melancholy look shows she does not live there. Demetrius, the grammarian, finding in the Temple of Delphi a knot of philosophers chattering together, said to them: "Either I am much deceived, or, by your cheerful and pleasant countenances, you

Study should not be made difficult.

are engaged in no very deep discourse." [38] To this, one of them, Heracleon, the Megarean, replied: "It is for such as puzzle their brains inquiring whether the future tense of βάλλω shall be spelled with a double λ, or who hunt after the derivation of the comparatives χεῖρον and βέλτιον, and the superlatives χείριστον and βέλτιστον, to knit their brows while discussing their subject. Philosophical discourses always amuse and cheer those that treat of them, and never deject people or make them sad."

> Deprendas animi tormenta latentis in ægro
> Corpore, deprendas et gaudia: sumit utrumque
> Inde habitum facies.[39]

> ("For still we find
> The face the unerring index of the mind,
> And as this feels or fancies joys or woes,
> That pales with anguish, or with rapture glows.")

The mind that harbours philosophy ought by reason of her sound health to make the body sound and healthy too. She ought to make her tranquillity and satisfaction shine, and her contentment ought to fashion the outward behaviour to her own mould, to fortify it with a graceful confidence, an active and joyous carriage, and a serene and contented countenance. The most certain sign of wisdom is a continual cheerfulness. Her state is like that of things in the regions above the moon, always clear and serene. It is *Baroco* and *Baralipton*[40] that make their followers so base and ill-favoured, and not philosophy, whom they know only by hearsay. It is she who calms and appeases the storms of the soul, and teaches misery, famine, and sickness to laugh, not because of some imaginary epicycles, but by natural and manifest reasons. Philosophy aims at nothing but virtue, which is not, as the Schoolmen say, situated upon the summit of a steep, rugged, and inaccessible precipice. On the contrary, those who have approached her say she is seated in a fair, fruitful, and flourishing plain, whence, as from a high watch tower, she surveys all things, to which any one may come if he knows the way, through shady, green, and sweet-scented walks; by a pleasant, easy, and smooth ascent, like that of the celestial arches. Some who are not acquainted with this supreme, beautiful, and courageous virtue, this implacable enemy to anxiety, sorrow, fear, and constraint, have followed their own weak imagination, and have created this ridiculous, this sorrowful, terrible counterfeit of it, placed it upon a solitary rock, and made of it a hobgoblin to frighten people who dare approach.

Now the tutor whom I would have, knowing it to be his duty to arouse affection as well as reverence for virtue, should teach his pupil that the poets [41] have always accommodated themselves to public feeling, and will therefore impress upon his charge that the gods have planted far more toil in the avenues which lead to pleasure than in those which will take him to wisdom. When the pupil begins once to apprehend this the tutor should present to him for a mistress a Bradamante or an Angelica—[42] a natural, active, generous, manly beauty, instead of soft, artificial, simpering, and affected charms: the one in the habit of an heroic youth with glittering helmet on her brow, the other tricked out with curls and ribbons. He will then judge whether his affection be brave and manly, and quite contrary to that of the effeminate shepherd of Phrygia.

<small>The practice of virtue is pleasurable.</small>

Such a tutor will make his pupil feel that the height and value of true virtue consist in the facility, utility, and pleasure of its exercise; so far from difficult that children as well as men, the simple as well as the wise, may make it their own; and that by order and good conduct, not by force, is virtue to be acquired. Socrates, her

<small>Office of true virtue.</small>

first favourite, was so averse to all manner of violence as to throw it all aside and naturally to slip into her path of progress. Virtue is the foster-mother of all human pleasures, who, in rendering them just, renders them also pure and permanent; in moderating them keeps them in breath and appetite. By refusing some, she whets our appetite for those she allows, and, like a kind and liberal mother, gives all that Nature requires even to satiety, if not to surfeit. We ought not to say that the regimen that stops the toper before he has killed himself, the glutton before he has ruined his stomach, the debauchee before he needs a surgeon, is an enemy to pleasure. If the ordinary fortune fail, virtue does without, or frames another, wholly her own, not so fickle and unsteady. She can be rich, potent, and wise, and knows how to lie upon a soft and perfumed couch. She loves life, beauty, glory, and health. But her proper and peculiar office is to know how to make a wise use of all these good things, and how to part with them without concern—an office more noble than troublesome, but without which the whole course of life is unnatural, turbulent, and deformed. There it is, indeed, that men may justly represent those monsters upon rocks and precipices.

If the pupil should happen to be of such a contrary disposition that he prefers an idle tale to the true story of some noble expedition; who at the beat of the drum that excites the youthful ardour of his companions leaves that to follow another that calls to a bear dance or to tumbling, juggling tricks, or who does not find it more delightful to return all weary and dusty from a victorious combat than from a tennis game; for such a one I see no remedy [43] except to bind him as apprentice to make mince pies, even though he be the son of a duke. I believe with Plato, that children are to be placed in life not according to the condition of the father, but according to their own capacity. [44]

Children should be educated according to their ability.

Since it is philosophy that teaches us how to live, and since infancy as well as other ages finds there its lessons, why should it not be communicated to children?

Philosophy adapted to early instruction.

"Udum et molle lutum est; nunc, nunc properandus, et acri,
Figendus sine fine rota." [45]

("The clay is moist and soft; now, now make haste
And form the vessel, for the wheel turns fast.")

We are taught to live when our lives are almost over. A hundred students have become diseased before they are ready to read Aristotle's Treatise on Temperance. Cicero said that though he should live two men's ages, he should never find leisure to study lyric poets. I find the Sophists yet more deplorably unprofitable. The youth we would train has little time to spare; he owes but the first fifteen or sixteen years of his life to his tutor, the remainder is due to action. Let us employ that short time in necessary instruction. Away with your crabbed, logical subtleties; they are abuses, things by which our lives can never be made better. Take the plain discourse of philosophy, first learn how to choose, then how to apply. Philosophy has discourses equally proper for children and old age.[46] Taught in the proper manner, they are more easily understood than one of Boccaccio's tales. A child first weaned is more capable of learning them than of learning to read and write.

I am inclined to think with Plutarch, that Aristotle did not trouble his great pupil so much with syllogisms or with geometry as with precepts concerning valour, prowess, magnanimity, temperance, and the contempt of fear. With such training Aristotle sent him, while yet a boy, with no more than thirty thousand

<small>Aristotle's training of Alexander.</small>

foot, four thousand horse, and forty thousand crowns, to conquer the whole world. As for the other arts and sciences, Alexander, he says, highly honoured them and commended their excellence, but did not care to practice them himself.

" Petite hinc, juvenesque senesque,
   Finem animo certum, miserisque viatica canis."⁴⁷

("Seek there both old and young, from truths like these,
   That certain aim which life's last cares may ease.")

Epicurus, in the beginning of his letter to Menœceus, says that "neither the youngest should refuse to philosophize, nor the eldest grow weary of it."⁴⁸ Who does otherwise tacitly implies that either the time of living happily is not yet come or is already past. Yet, for all that, I would not have this pupil of ours imprisoned and made a slave to his book, nor have him acquire the morose and melancholy disposition of a sour, ill-natured pedant. I would not have his spirit cowed and subdued by tormenting him fourteen or fifteen hours a day, as some do, making a pack horse of him. Neither should I think it good to encourage an abnormal taste for books, if it be discovered that he is too much addicted to reading. Too

Danger of too much book-study.

much study diverts him from better employment, and renders him unfit for the society of men. Many a time have I seen men totally useless on account of an immoderate thirst for knowledge. Carneades[49] was so besotted with it that he could not find time to cut his nails or comb his hair. Neither would I have the noble manners of my pupil spoiled by the incivility and barbarity of other people. French wisdom was anciently turned into a proverb, "Early, but does not continue." Nothing can be prettier than the children of France, but they ordinarily deceive the hopes and expectations of parents, and grow up to be men of very ordinary ability. I have heard men of good understanding insist that these colleges of ours make our children the animals they turn out to be.[50] But to our young friend, a closet, a garden, the table, his bed, solitude, company, morning and evening—all hours and all places of study shall be the same.

Philosophy, as the former of judgment and manner, should be his principal lesson, and should regulate everything. Isocrates the orator was once at a feast and invited to speak of his art. "It is not now a time," said he, "to do what I can do, and what I should do I can

Philosophy in its relation to life the chief study.

not do."[51] Every one commended his answer. To make orations or to enter into rhetorical dispute, in a company met together to laugh and to enjoy good cheer, would be very unreasonable and improper. As much might be said of all other learning. But as to philosophy, especially that part which treats of man and his duties, it is the unanimous opinion of all wise men that, on account of the sweetness of her conversation, she ought to be admitted to all sports and entertainments. Plato having invited her to his feast, we see in what a gentle and obliging manner she accommodated herself both to time and place, and entertained the company in a discourse of the sublimest nature.

"Æque pauperibus prodest, locupletibus æque,
Æque neglectum pueris senibusque nocebit."[52]

("It profits poor and rich alike; and when
Neglected, to old and young is hurtful then.")

By this method of instruction my young pupil will be much better employed than those who are at college. The steps we take in walking to and fro in a gallery, though they are three times as many, do not weary us so much as those we take in a formal journey; so our les-

The whole man should be trained.

sons, occurring as it were accidentally, without any set obligation of time and place, and falling in naturally with every action, will be learned as a pleasure, not as a task. Our very exercises and recreations, running, wrestling, dancing, hunting, riding, and fencing, will be a part of his study. I would have his manners, behaviour, and bearing cultivated at the same time with his mind. It is not the mind, it is not the body we are training: it is the man, and we must not divide him into two parts. Plato says we should not fashion one without the other, but make them draw together like two horses harnessed to a coach. By this saying would it not indicate that he would rather give more care to the body, believing that the mind is benefited at the same time?[53]

As to the rest, this method ought to be carried on with a firm gentleness, quite contrary to the practice of our pedants, who, instead of tempting and alluring children to study, present nothing before them but rods and ferules, horror and cruelty. Away with this violence! away with this compulsion! nothing, I believe, more dulls and degenerates a well-born nature. If you would have a child fear shame and punishment, do not harden him to

<small>Study to be made pleasant, but effeminacy avoided.</small>

them. Accustom him to heat and cold, to wind and sun, and to dangers that he ought to despise. Wean him from all effeminacy in eating and drinking, clothes and lodging, that he may not be a gay fellow, a dude, but a hardy, sinewy, and vigorous young man. I have been of this opinion all my life, and still hold to it.

The strict government of our colleges has always displeased me;[54] less harm would have *College discipline too rigorous.* been done had they erred on the indulgent side. They are mere jails, where youths are corrupted by being punished before they have done any wrong. Go into one of these institutions during lesson hours, and you hear nothing but the outcries of boys being punished and the thundering of pedagogues drunk with fury. A pretty way it is to tempt these tender and timorous souls to love their books—a furious countenance, rod in hand! O wicked and pernicious manner of teaching! Besides, Quintilian[55] has well observed that this insolent authority is often attended by dangerous consequences, particularly in the matter of punishments.

Make school-life pleasant. How much more respectable it would be to see our classrooms strewn with green boughs and flowers than with bloody birch rods. Were it left to my ordering, I should paint the school with pictures of joy and gladness, Flora and the Graces, as the philosopher Speusippus[56] did his. Where their profit is there should also be their pleasure. Such viands as are proper and wholesome for children should be seasoned with sugar, and such as are dangerous with gall. It is interesting to see how careful Plato is, in framing the laws, to provide for the recreation of the youths of his city.[57] He enlarges upon the races, sports, leaps, songs, and dances; he said antiquity had given the ordering of these to Apollo, Minerva, and the Muses. He insists upon a thousand exercises for both mind and body, but says very little of the learned sciences, and seems to recommend poetry only on account of the music.

All oddity of manner and self-consciousness should be avoided as obnoxious to society.

<small>Singularity of manners to be avoided.</small> Who is not astonished at a man like Demophoön, steward of Alexander the Great, who perspired in the shade and shivered in the sun. I have seen those who would run from the smell of apples quicker than from an arquebuse; others are afraid of a mouse; others become sick at the sight of cream; others faint at seeing a feather bed shaken. There was Germanicus

who could endure neither the sight nor the crowing of a cock. Perhaps there may be some occult cause for aversions of this kind, but, in my opinion, a man might conquer them if he took them in time. Training has been effectual in my case; excepting beer, my appetite accommodates itself to all kinds of diet.

Young bodies are supple, one should therefore bend them to fit all fashions and customs. **Cultivate adaptability.** Provided he can restrain the appetite and the will within limits, let a young man accustom himself to all nations and companies, even to debauchery and excess, if he do so simply out of regard to the customs of a place. Let him be able to do everything, but love to do nothing but what is good. The philosophers themselves do not commend Calisthenes for losing the favour of his master Alexander, by refusing to pledge him in a glass of wine. Let the young man laugh, carouse, and debauch with his prince; I would have him, even in his excesses, surpass his companions in ability and vigour, so that he may not refrain from such pleasures through lack of power or knowledge, but for lack of will. "Multum interest, utrum peccare aliquis nolit, aut nesciat."[58] ("There is a vast difference between forbearing to sin and not knowing how to sin.")

I once complimented a lord—as free from these excesses as any man in France—by asking him before a large company how many times he had been drunk in Germany while there on a special mission for his Majesty. He took it as I intended he should, and answered, "Three times," telling us the circumstances. I know some who, for want of this faculty of adjustment, have great difficulty in treating with that nation. I have often admired the wonderful versatility of Alcibiades, who could adapt himself to any customs without injury to his health. He could outdo the Persians in pomp and luxury, the Lacedæmonians in austerity and frugality, and could be as temperate in Sparta as voluptuous in Ionia.

"Omnis Aristippum decuit color, et status et res." [59]

("Old Aristippus every dress became,
In every state and circumstance the same.")

Such a one I would make my pupil.

"Quem duplici panno patientia velat,
Mirabor, vitæ via si conversa decebit.
. . . .
Personamque feret non inconcinnus utramque." [60]

("But that a man whom patience taught to wear
A coat that's patched, should even learn to bear
A changed life with decency and grace,
May justly, I confess, our wonder raise.")

These are my lessons, and he who puts them in practice will reap more advantage than he who only listens to them.

"The gods forbid," says one in Plato, "that to philosophize should be only to read a great many books and to learn the arts."

Learn to live.

"Hanc amplissimam omnium artium bene vivendi disciplinam, vita magis quam literis, persecuti sunt."[61] ("The best of all arts—that of living well—they followed in their lives rather than in their learning.") Leo, prince of the Philiasians, asked Heraclides[62] Ponticus of what art or science he made profession. "I know," said he, "neither art nor science, but I am a philosopher." Some one reproved Diogenes for being ignorant and meddling with philosophy. He answered, "I therefore pretend to it with so much the more reason." Hegesias once requested Diogenes to read him a certain book, at which the philosopher said: "You are an amusing person. You choose figs that are true and natural, not those that are painted; why do you not also choose exercises which are natural and true rather than those written?"[63]

A boy should not so much memorize his lesson as practice it. Let him repeat it in his actions. We shall discover if there be pru-

OF THE EDUCATION OF CHILDREN.

dence in him by his undertakings; goodness and justice, by his deportment; grace and judgment, by his speaking; fortitude, by his sickness; temperance, by his pleasures; order, by the management of his affairs; and indifference, by his palate, whether what he eats and drinks be flesh or fish, wine or water. "Qui disciplinam suam non ostentationem scientiæ, sed legem vitæ putet; quique obtemperet ipsi sibi; et decretis pareat." ("Who considers his own learning not as idle show, but as a law and rule of life, and obeys his own decrees and follows the course laid out by himself.") The conduct of our lives is the true mirror of our doctrine. Zeuxidamus, to one who asked him why the Lacedæmonians did not write down their laws of chivalry and have their young men read them, replied, "Because we would rather accustom them to deeds than to writings." With such a one compare, after fifteen or sixteen years of study, one of our college Latinists, who has thrown away all his time in learning to speak. The world is nothing but babble, and I have never yet seen a man who did not say too much rather than too little. And yet half our life goes this way. We are kept four or five years learning words and tacking

"Actions speak louder than words."

them together into phrases, as many more to combine these into paragraphs, and another five is spent in learning how to weave them together into an intricate and rhetorical style. Let us leave such work to those who make it a trade.

Going one day to Orleans, I met in the plain this side of Cléry two pedants travelling to Bordeaux. They were about fifty paces apart, and a considerable distance behind I saw a troop of horse with a gentleman at the head of them, the late Monsieur le Comte de la Rochefoucauld. One of my servants inquired of the first of these pedants who it was that was coming. Not having seen the train, and thinking my servant meant his companion, he answered, "He is not a gentleman, but a grammarian, and I am a logician." On the contrary, we do not wish to make a grammarian, nor a logician, but a gentleman, so let us leave them to throw away their time; we have other business.

<small>Pedantry ridiculed.</small>

Let our pupil be furnished with things—words will come only too fast; if they do not come readily, he will reach after them. I have heard some make excuses because they can not express themselves, and pretend to have their heads full of a great

<small>Things before words.</small>

OF THE EDUCATION OF CHILDREN.

many very fine things which for want of words they can not bring out. Do you know what I think of such people? I think they are nothing but shadows of imperfect images; they have no thoughts within, and consequently can not bring any out. They do not know themselves what they are trying to say, and if you notice how they haggle and stammer, you will soon conclude their pretensions to learning are downright false. For my part I hold, and Socrates is positive in it, that whoever has in his mind a clear and vivid idea, will express it well enough in one way or another; and if he be dumb, by signs.

> "Verbaque provisam rem non invita sequentur."[65]
>
> ("When matter they foreknow,
> Words voluntarily flow.")

And another as poetically says in prose, "Quum res animum occupavere, verba ambiunt."[66] ("When things are once in the mind words offer themselves.") And this other, "Ipsæ res verba rapiunt."[67] ("The things themselves force words to express them.") He knows no more of ablative, conjunctive, substantive or grammar than his lackey or a fishwife of the Petit-Pont; and yet he will give you your fill of talk, and perhaps stumble as little in his language as the best masters of art in France. He knows no rhetoric, nor how in a preface to capture the good-will of the courteous reader; nor does he greatly care to know. Indeed, all this fine sort of painting is easily obscured by the lustre of simple truth; these ingenious flourishes serve only to amuse the vulgar who are themselves incapable of more solid and nutritive diet, as Aper very plainly shows in Tacitus.[68] The ambassadors of Samos, prepared with a long eloquent oration, came to Cleomenes, King of Sparta, to urge him to make war against the tyrant Polycrates. The king heard their harangue with much gravity and patience, and then gave them this short answer: "As to your exordium, I remember it not; the middle of your speech I have forgotten; and as to your conclusions, I will not do as you desire."[69] This was a fine answer, I think, and no doubt the learned orators were much mortified. Here is another instance: The Athenians were to choose one of two architects for a great building they proposed to erect. The first, an affected fellow, offered his services in a long premeditated discourse, and by his oratory inclined the people in his favor; the other simply remarked, "Lords of Athens, what this man has said, I will do."[70]

OF THE EDUCATION OF CHILDREN. 71

When Cicero's eloquence was at its height many were struck with admiration; but Cato only laughed at it, saying, "We have a pleasant Consul."[71] A cunning argument or a witty saying, whether before or after a speech, is never out of place. If it fits in neither with what went before nor comes after, it is good in itself. I am not one of those who think good rhyme makes good poetry. Let the writer make a long syllable short, if he will, it is no great matter. If the thinking be true and good judgment has been exercised, I will say of such a one, Here is a good poet but a poor versifier.

"Emunctæ naris, durus componere versus."[72]

("He rallied with a gay and easy air,
But rude his numbers and his style severe.")

Again, Horace says that a man should divest his work of all artificiality.

"Tempora certa modosque, et quod prius ordine
  verbum est
Posterius facias, præponens ultima primis,
. . . .
Invenias etiam disjecti membra poetæ."[73]

("Let tense and mood and words be all misplaced,
 Those last that should be first, those first the last;
 Though all things be thus shuffled out of frame,
 You'll find the poet's fragments not to blame.")

He will receive no censure thereby; the work will be fine in itself. This is what Menander meant in his answer to a friend who reproved him for not having a word of the comedy he had promised in a few days. "It is all ready," he said, "all but the verses." Having arranged the plot and disposed of the scenes, he cared little for the rest. Since Ronsard and Du Bellay have given reputation to our French poetry, every little dabbler swells his words as high and makes cadences almost as harmonious as they. "Plus sonat, quam valet."[74] ("More sound than sense.") There were never so many poetasters as now; but though they find it no hard matter to rhyme nearly as well as their masters, yet they fall altogether short of the rich description of the one, and the delicate invention of the other.

Invention the true test of poetry.

But what will become of our young gentleman if he be attacked with the sophistic subtlety of some syllogism? "A Westphalian ham makes a man drink; drink quenches thirst; therefore a Westphalian ham quenches thirst."[75] Why, let him laugh at it, and thereby show more sense than if he attempted to answer it. Or let him borrow this

Sophistical subtleties unworthy of serious attention.

OF THE EDUCATION OF CHILDREN.

pleasant evasion from Aristippus: "Why should I untie that which, even bound, gives me so much trouble?"[76] A person once using these delicate jugglings against Cleanthes, Chrysippus cut him short with, "Reserve these tricks for children, and do not by such fooleries divert the serious thoughts of a man of years."[77] If these ridiculous subtleties—"Contorta et aculeata sophismata" ("Intricate and stinging sophisms ")[78]—are designed to mislead, they are then dangerous; but if they only make him laugh, I do not see why a man need be fortified against them.

Some are so foolish as to go a mile out of their way to bring in a fine word. "Aut qui non verba rebus aptant, sed res extrinsecus arcessunt quibus verba conveniant."[79] ("Who do not fit words to the subject, but seek outside matter to fit the words.") And as another says, "Qui alicujus verbi decore placentis vocentur ad id, quod non proposuerant scribere."[80] ("Who by their fondness for a fine-sounding word are tempted to write something they did not intend to write.") I, for my part, rather bring in a fine sentence by head and shoulders to fit my purpose, than divert my design to hunt after a sentence. It is for words to serve

Style and matter should harmonize.

and to follow matter, and let Gascon come in play where French will not do. I would have things so possess the imagination of him that hears, that he will have no remembrance at all of the words. I like a natural, simple, and unaffected manner of speaking and writing; a sinewy and significant way of expressing one's self, not so elegant and artificial as prompt and vehement. "Hæc demum sapiet dictio, quæ feriet."[81] ("The language which strikes the mind will please it.") I prefer a style rather hard than tedious, free from affectation, irregular, and bold; not like a pedant's, a preacher's, or a pleader's, but rather a soldier-like style, as Suetonius[82] calls that of Julius Cæsar, though I see no reason why he should call it so.

Avoid affectation in dress and language.
I have been ready enough to imitate the negligent garb which is observable among the young men of our time, to wear my cloak on one shoulder, my hat on one side, and one stocking somewhat more disorderly than the other, thereby expressing a sort of manly disdain for these exotic ornaments. But I find carelessness of even greater use in speaking. All affectation, particularly in the French gaiety and freedom, is ungraceful in a courtier; and

in a monarchy every gentleman ought to be trained according to the court model, which requires an easy and natural negligence. I do not like a piece of cloth where the seams and knots are to be seen, and as little do I like in a well-proportioned man to be able to tell all the bones and veins. "Quæ veritati operam dat oratio, incomposita sit et simplex."[83] "Quis accurate loquitur nisi qui vult putide loqui?"[84] ("Let the language which is dedicated to truth be plain and unaffected.") ("Who speaks like a pedant but one who means thereby to speak offensively?") The eloquence which calls attention to itself, injures the subject it would advance. In our dress it is ridiculous effeminacy to distinguish ourselves by a peculiar fashion; so in language, to study new phrases and to affect words that are not in current use proceeds from a childish and scholastic ambition. As for me, may I never use any other language than what will be understood in the markets of Paris! Aristophanes was out of the way when he reproved Epicurus, for his simplicity and the design of his oratory, which was only a perspicuity of speech.[85]

This imitation of words by its own facility immediately disperses itself through a whole people. But the imitation of judgment in applying these words is of slower growth. Most readers when they find a robe like their own imagine it contains a body like their own; but force and sinews are not to be borrowed, though the attire may be. Most of those I converse with speak the same language I here write, but whether they think the same thoughts I can not say. The Athenians, says Plato, study length and elegance of speaking; the Lacedæmonians affect brevity; but the people of Crete aim more at richness of thought than at fertility of speech, and these are the best.

Imitation of words easy, of thoughts difficult.

Zeno used to say he had two kinds of disciples: one he called φιλόλογος, curious to learn things, and these were his favourites; the other he called λογόφιλος, who cared for nothing but words. Not that good language is anything but commendable, but it is not so excellent nor so necessary as some would make it. I am shocked that our whole life should be spent in nothing else. I would first understand my own language, and then that of my neighbours with whom I have most to do. No doubt Greek and Latin are great ornaments, but we pay too much for them. I will tell you how they may be gotten better,

OF THE EDUCATION OF CHILDREN. 77

cheaper, and much more quickly than by the ordinary way; it was tried upon myself, and anyone may make use of the method who wishes to do so.

My late father having made most careful inquiry of the wisest men as to the best method of education, was cautioned by them against the systems then in use. They believed that the long time required to learn the languages of those people who were born to them was the sole reason we can never attain to the grandeur of soul and perfection of knowledge of the ancient Greeks and Romans. I do not think, however, that is the only cause. The expedient my father found out was this: In my infancy, and before I began to speak, he committed me to the care of a German (who has since died, a famous physician in France) totally ignorant of our language but very well versed in Latin. This man, whom my father had sent for and paid a large salary, had me continually with him. He was assisted by two Germans of inferior learning, but none of them conversed in any other language but Latin. As for the rest of the family, it was an inviolable rule that neither himself nor my mother, nor the servants, should speak any-

Montaigne's early education.

thing in my company but such Latin words as everyone had learned to talk with me. You can hardly imagine what an advantage this proved to be to the whole family. My father and my mother learned Latin enough to understand it perfectly well, and to speak it to such a degree as was necessary for ordinary use; as well also did the servants who were most frequently with me. In short, we were all so Latinized that it overflowed to the neighbouring towns, where it yet remains in several Latin appellations of artisans and their tools. As for myself, I was more than six years of age before I understood either French or Perigordian any more than Arabic.[86] I had learned to speak as pure Latin as my master himself without art, book, grammar or precept, whipping or a single tear. If, for example, they were to give me a theme after the college fashion, they gave it to the others in French, but to me in bad Latin, to turn it into pure and good. Nicholas Grouchy, who wrote De Comitiis Romanorum; William Guerente, who has written a Commentary on Aristotle; George Buchanan, the famous Scottish poet; and Mark Antony Murel, whom both France and Italy have acknowledged as the best orator of his time—my domestic tutor—have all of them told me that even in my infancy I understood Latin so well they were afraid to talk with me. Buchanan, whom I afterward saw attending upon the late Marshal de Brissac, told me he intended to write a treatise upon Education, taking for his model my own education. He was then tutor to the young Count de Brissac, who afterward became so valiant and so brave a gentleman.

As to Greek, of which I have but a smattering, my father proposed to teach it by a new device, making of it a sort of sport and recreation.[87] We tossed our declensions and conjugations to and fro, after the manner of those who by certain games at table and chess learn geometry and arithmetic. Among other things, he had been advised to make me enjoy study and duty; to accept them of my own free will, and to educate my soul in all liberty and delight, without any severity or constraint. He believed almost to superstition that it was wrong to arouse children suddenly from a sound sleep, in which they are more deeply lost than we are. I was always awakened by the sound of some musical instrument, a special musician being provided for that purpose.

Use of motor side.

By these examples alone you may judge of the prudence and affection of my good father, who is not to be blamed because he did not reap fruits commensurate with his exquisite toil and careful culture. For this result there are two reasons. First, a sterile and improper soil. Though of a strong, healthy constitution, a gentle and tractable disposition, I was heavy, idle, and sluggish. They could not arouse me to any exercise or recreation, nor even get me out to play. What I saw, I saw clearly enough, and, despite this laziness, possessed a lively imagination and opinions far above my years. I had a slow mind that would go no faster than it was led, weak creative power, and, above all, a poor memory. With all these defects it is not strange my father could make but little of me. Secondly, like those who, impatient of a long and steady cure, submit to all sorts of nostrums and listen to every quack, so the good man, fearful of his plan, and having no longer the persons he had brought out of Italy, allowed himself to be overruled by the common opinion which always follows the lead of what goes before, like cranes, and sent me at six years of age to the College of Gui-

Montaigne's disposition accounts for the partial failure of this educational scheme.

OF THE EDUCATION OF CHILDREN. 81

enne, at that time the best and most flourishing in France. Even there he provided the most able tutor, and obtained many privileges for me contrary to college rules. And yet with all these precautions it was a college still. My Latin immediately grew corrupt, and by discontinuance I lost all use of it. This new plan of education, therefore, was of no benefit to me except to skip me over some of the lower classes and place me in the highest. I left college when I was thirteen, but without any improvement that I can boast of, though I finished the whole course, as they call it.

The first thing that gave me any taste for books was the pleasure I took in reading the fables of Ovid's Metamorphoses.[88] When but seven or eight years old I would steal away from all other diversions to read them. They were written in my own natural language, the easiest tales I was acquainted with, and the subject was suited to my age and capacity. So carefully was I taught that I knew nothing of Lancelot du Lac, Amadis de Gaul, Huon of Bordeaux, and such idle, time-consuming, and pernicious books in which most children delight. To this day I do not know what those

The tale the best literature for children.

books contain. Of course, I thought little of my prescribed lessons, and right here it was greatly to my advantage to have a sensible tutor wise enough to connive at this and other irregularities of the same nature. In this way I ran through Virgil's Æneid, then Terence, then Plautus, and some Italian comedies, allured by the pleasure of the subject. On the other hand, had my tutor been so foolish as to deprive me of this amusement, I verily believe I would have brought nothing away from college but a hatred of books, as most of our young gentlemen do. He was very discreet about that business, apparently taking no notice, and whetting my appetite by allowing me only such time for this reading as I could steal from my regular studies.

<small>Montaigne's inaction.</small> The chief thing my father expected from those to whom he committed my education, was affability of manner and a good disposition. To tell the truth, I had few faults except laziness and a want of mettle. The fear was not that I should do ill, but that I should do nothing. No one expected that I would be wicked, but most thought I would be useless. They foresaw idleness, but no malice in my nature; and so it happens. The complaints I

OF THE EDUCATION OF CHILDREN. 83

hear of myself are these: "He is idle, cold in the offices of friendship and relationship, and remiss in those of the public; he is too particular, he is too proud." My worst enemies do not say: "Why has he taken such a thing? why has he not paid such a one?" but, "Why does he not give something once in a while?" No doubt I should take it for a favour that men expect no greater effects of supererogation then these. But they are unjust to exact from me what I do not owe, far more rigorously than they exact from others what they do owe. By condemning me they efface the gratification of the act and deprive me of the pleasure due. Anything from my hand should be of greater value, since I am so little disposed that way. I can the more freely dispose of my fortune since it is mine, and of myself since I am my own. If I were good at blazoning my own actions, I could repel these reproaches, and show that people are not so much offended because I do little, as because I do less than I might. Yet, in spite of this strange disposition of mine, I have never failed to have clear judgment concerning those things I could understand, though I believe I never could have made my mind submit to anything by violence or force.

Shall I here tell you of a peculiarity of my youth? I had great boldness and assurance of countenance, to which was added a flexibility of voice and gesture. "Alter ab undecimo tum me jam acceperat annus"[89] ("I had hardly entered upon my twelfth year") when I played the chief parts in the Latin tragedies of Buchanan, Guerente, and Muret, that were acted in our college of Guienne in great state. Andreas Goveanus, our principal, as in everything he undertook, was the best actor of Latin plays in France, and I was looked upon as one of his chief assistants. This is an exercise I do not disapprove of in young gentlemen, and I have seen our princes perform such parts in person well and commendably. In Greece, people of the highest station were allowed to profess and to make a trade of acting. "Aristoni tragico actori rem aperit; huic et genus et fortuna honesta erant; nec ars quia nihil tale apud Græcos pudori est ea deformabat."[90] ("He imparted this matter to Aristo the tragedian, a man of good family and fortune. Nevertheless, neither of them received any harm, for nothing of that kind is considered a disparagement in Greece.") I have always taxed persons with impertinence who condemn these

Montaigne approves of the stage.

entertainments, and with injustice those who refuse such comedies as are worth seeing, to come into our towns and begrudge the people that public amusement. A sensible plan of government takes care to assemble citizens not only to the solemn duties of devotion, but also to sports and spectacles. Society and friendship are augmented by it; and, besides, can there possibly be afforded a more orderly diversion than one which is performed in the sight of everyone, and often in the presence of the supreme magistrate himself? I, for my part, think it desirable that the prince should sometimes gratify his people at his own expense, out of paternal kindness, as it were. In large cities theatres should be erected for such entertainments, if for nothing more than to divert people from private and worse actions.

To return to my subject: There is nothing like alluring the appetite and affection, otherLearning should be made alluring and permanent. wise you make nothing but so many asses laden with books. By virtue of the lash, you give them a pocketful of learning to keep, whereas you should not only lodge it with them, but marry it to them, and make it a part of their very minds and souls.

8

OF PEDANTRY.

Book I, Chapter XXIV.

Pedantry despised by ancients and moderns.

WHEN a boy, I was often greatly distressed to see in Italian farces a pedant always brought in for the fool of the play, and that the title of magister was held in so little reverence. They were my teachers, and how could I help being jealous of their honour and reputation? I found comfort in the fact, however, that there is great difference between the common sort and men of finer thread; both in judgment and knowledge they differ greatly.[91] But what puzzled me most was that the wisest men most despised them; witness our famous Du Bellay. "Mais ie hay par sur tout un scavoir pedantesque." ("But of all sorts of learning, I most hate that of a pedant.") And so they felt in ancient times, for Plutarch says that Grecian and Scholar were terms of contempt among the Romans. Since I have come to years of more discretion I find they had much reason for their judgment, and that

"Magis magnos clericos non sunt magis magnos sapientes."[92] ("The greatest clerks are not the wisest men.") From this it would appear that a mind enriched with the knowledge of so many things does not become ready and sprightly, and that a vulgar understanding can exist by the side of all the reasoning and judgment the world has collected and stored up without benefit thereby. One of our greatest princesses once said to me, in speaking of a certain person, "It must be necessary to squeeze and crowd one's own brains into a smaller compass to make room for such large portions of the brains of others." I might say that as plants are choked and drowned with too much moisture, and lamps with too much oil, so is the active mind overwhelmed with too much study and matter. The mind is embarrassed and perplexed with the diversity of things, and is bowed down and rendered useless by the pressure of this weight. But the argument is weak; it is quite otherwise, the mind stretches and dilates itself the more it fills.

In ancient times we find men excellent at public business, great captains, great statesmen, and yet very learned. On the other hand, mere philosophers, men retired from all public affairs, have been laughed at by the comic writers of their own time, their opinions and singular manners making them appear, to men of another method of living, ridiculous and absurd. If at any time you should wish to make these philosophers judges of a lawsuit, or of the actions of a man, they are ready at once to take it upon themselves. They begin to examine if he has life, if he has motion, if a man be anything more than an ox;[93] what it is to do and to suffer; and what animals, law and justice are. Do they speak of the magistrate, or to him? It is with a rude, irreverent, and indecent liberty. Do they hear a prince or a king commended for his virtue? They make no more of him than of a shepherd or an idle swain, who busies himself only about milking, and shearing his flocks; and this in a ruder manner than even the shepherd himself would do it. Do you consider any man the greater for being lord of two thousand acres? They laugh at such a pittance, laying claim themselves to the whole world for their possession. Do you boast of your nobility and blood, being descended from seven successive, rich ancestors? They will look upon you with an eye of contempt, as

Ability versus mere learning and material circumstances.

men who have not the right idea of the universal image of Nature, and who do not consider how many predecessors every one of us has had, rich, poor, kings, slaves, Greeks, and barbarians. Though you were the fiftieth descendant from Hercules, they look upon it as a great vanity to value so highly that which is only a gift of fortune. In this way they incur the dislike of common men, who consider them ignorant of first principles, as presumptuous and insolent.

But this Platonic picture is far different from the modern idea of these pedants. Those were envied for raising themselves above the common sort of men; for despising the ordinary actions and offices of life; for having a particular and inimitable way of living, and for using bombastic and obsolete language quite different from the ordinary way of speaking. But our pedants are condemned for being as much below the usual man as they are incapable of public employment; for leading the life and comforming themselves to the mean and vile manners of the vulgar. "Odi homines ignavos opere, philosophos sententia."[94] ("I hate men who are fools in working and philosophers in speaking.")

Ancient and modern pedants contrasted.

The true philosophers, if they were great in knowledge, were yet much greater in action.

<small>True philosophers are great in action.</small>

It is said of Archimedes, the geometrician of Syracuse, being disturbed from his contemplation to put some of his skill in practice for the defence of his country, that he suddenly constructed prodigious and dreadful engines, that wrought effects beyond all human expectations. Nevertheless, he himself disdained all this mechanical work, thinking in this he had violated the dignity of his art, of which these performances were but trivial experiments. Philosophers generally, whenever they have been required to show the proof of action, have been seen to fly so high as to make it very evident that their souls were strangely elevated and enriched with the knowledge of things.

Some philosophers, seeing the reins of government in the hands of ignorant and unskilful men, have avoided all interest in the management of affairs.

<small>Some philosophers who refused public office.</small>

Some one who demanded of Crates how long it would be necessary to philosophize, received this answer, "Till our armies are no longer commanded by fools."[95] Heraclitus resigned the throne[96] to his brother. The Ephesians reproached him that he spent his time in playing with children before the temple. "Is it not better to do so," he replied, "than to govern in your company?"[97] Others, having their imagination above the thoughts of the world and fortune, have looked upon the tribunals of justice, and even the thrones of kings, with an eye of contempt and scorn. Empedocles refused the throne that the Agrigentines offered him.[98]

Thales, once inveighing against the pains men take to become rich, was told by one of the company that he was like the fox who found fault with what he could not obtain. For the jest's sake he undertook to show them the contrary. For once he employed all his learning and capacity in the service of money-making, and in one year made as much as the others with all their industry could have raked together in the whole course of their lives.[99] Aristotle speaks of some one who called himself, Anaxagoras, and others of their profession, wise but not prudent, because they did not apply their study to profitable things. I do not quite understand this nice distinction, and it certainly will not excuse my pedants. The poverty with which they are content

The better-learned preferable to the more-learned.

would argue they are neither wise nor prudent. But leaving this reason aside, I think it is better to say that this poverty comes because they apply themselves in the wrong way to the study of science. As we are taught, it is no wonder that neither the scholar nor the master becomes, though more learned, the wiser or more fit for business. In plain truth, the care and the expense to which our parents put themselves aim at nothing but furnishing our heads with knowledge; not a word is said of judgment and virtue. If one pass by, the people cry out, "Oh, what a learned man!" and of another, "Oh, what a good man goes there!"[100] All turn their eyes and pay their respects to the former. There should be a third crier to call out, "Oh, the blockheads!" Men are apt to inquire, "Does such a one understand Greek and Latin? Is he a poet, or does he write prose?" But the main point, whether he be better or more discreet, we inquire into last. The question should be, Who is the better learned? rather than, Who is the more learned?

We labor and plot to stuff the memory and in the meantime leave the conscience and the understanding empty. And like birds which fly abroad to forage for grain and bring it home in their beaks, without tasting it themselves, to feed their young, so our pedants go picking knowledge here and there out of several authors, and hold it at tongue's end only to distribute it among their pupils. And right here I cannot help smiling to think how I am showing myself off as an example of this same sort of learning. I go here and there, culling out of several books those sentences which please me best, not to keep—for I have no memory to keep them in—but to transplant them into this; when, to say the truth, they are no more mine than in the first place. In my opinion, we are never wise except by present learning; not by that which is past, and as little by that which is to come.

Pedants neglect moral training.

But the worst of it is, their pupils are no better nourished by it than the pedants themselves. No deeper impression is made upon them than upon the pedants. It passes from hand to hand only to make a show, to be pleasant company, and to tell pretty stories; like counterfeit coin, of no other use or value but as counters to reckon with or set up at cards. "Apud alios loqui didicerunt non ipsi secum." [101] ("They have learned to speak to others, not to themselves.") "Non est lo-

Pupils no better than pedants.

quendum, sed gubernandum."[102] ("The thing is not to talk, but to govern.") Nature, to show there is nothing barbarous where she has the sole command, often in the least civilized nations produces excellent examples of wit. In this connection the Gascon proverb, derived from a reed-pipe, is very quaint and subtle: "Bouha prou bouha mas a remuda lous dits qu'em." ("You may blow till your eyes start out; but if once you stir your finger, the lesson will be at an end.") We can say, Cicero speaks thus; These were the ideas of Plato; These are the very words of Aristotle. A parrot could say as much. But what do we say that is our own? what can we do? how do we judge?

This puts me in mind of that rich Roman gentleman [103] who went to great expense to procure men possessing all sorts of knowledge, whom he had always attending his person, so that when, among his friends, he was speaking of any subject whatever, they supplied his place and furnished him, one with a sentence from Seneca, another with a verse of Homer, and so on. He fancied this knowledge to be his own, because it was contained in his servants' heads. There are many like him whose learning consists in having noble libraries.

Buying brains.

We take other men's knowledge and opinions upon trust, but we should make them our own. In this we are very much like the man who went to his neighbour's house to fetch some fire, and finding a very good one there, sat down to warm himself, forgetting to carry any home with him.[104] What good does it do us to have the stomach full of meat if it does not digest and become a part of us?—if it does not nourish and support us?[105] Learning without any experience made Lucullus a great leader.[106] Can we imagine he studied after this perfunctory manner? We allow ourselves to lean upon the arm of another, and so prejudice our own strength and vigour. Would I fortify myself against the fear of death? It must be at the expense of Seneca. Would I extract consolation for myself or my friend? I borrow it from Cicero. I might have found it in myself, had I been trained to make use of my reason. I have no use for this mendicant knowledge. For though we may become learned by other men's reading, a man can never be wise but by his own wisdom.

No learning of use but what we make our own.

"Μισῶ σοφιστὴν, ὅστις οὐχ αὑτῷ σοφός."[107]
("Who in his own concern's not wise,
 That man's wisdom I despise.")

Whence Ennius, "Nequidquam sapere sapientem qui ipse sibi prodesse non quiret."[106] ("That wise man knows nothing who can not benefit himself by his wisdom.") "Non enim paranda nobis solum, sed fruenda sapientia est."[109] ("For wisdom is not only to be acquired, but to be made use of.")

> Si cupidus, si
> Vanus et Euganea quantumvis mollior agna.[110]

("If covetous, if vain, or weaker than an Euganean lamb.")

Dionysius[111] laughed at the grammarians who cudgelled their brains to know the miseries of Ulysses and were ignorant of their own; at musicians who were so exact in tuning their instruments and never tuned their manners; and at orators who studied to declare what is justice, but never took care to do it. If the mind be not better disposed, if the judgment be no better settled, I would rather my student had spent his time at tennis, for at least his body would be in better health by that exercise. Look at him when he comes from school, after fifteen or sixteen years' study. Could there be anything more awkward, more unfit for company or employment? All he has is his

Schools furnish children with little real knowledge.

Latin and Greek, which have made him a more conceited blockhead than when he went from home. He should bring back a mind replete with sound literature, instead he brings a head swelled and puffed out with vain and empty shreds and snatches of learning, and there is really nothing more in him than he had before.

Plato speaks of the Sophists as those who pretend to be useful to mankind, and yet alone of all men living do not improve what is committed to them, as a mason or a carpenter would, but make it worse and then require pay. So it is with our pedants, their cousins-german. If the rule which Protagoras[112] proposed to his pupils were followed, either that they should give him his price, or declare upon oath in the temple how much they valued the profit they had received under his instruction, and satisfy him accordingly, our pedagogues would find themselves disappointed, especially if they were to be judged by the testimony of my experience. Our common Perigordian patois pleasantly calls these pretenders to learning, "*lettre-ferits*," letter marked; men upon whom letters have been stamped by the blow of a mallet, as it were. And in truth, for the most

Pretenders to learning.

part, they appear to have a soft spot in their skull, and to be deprived of common sense. You see the husbandman and the cobbler go simply and plainly about their business, speaking only of what they know and understand. On the other hand, these fellows in seeking to make a parade and flourish with this ridiculous knowledge, that floats in their brains, are perpetually perplexing and entangling themselves in their own nonsense. They speak fine words sometimes, it is true, but somebody that is wise must apply them. They are wonderfully acquainted with Galen, but not at all with the disease of the patient. They stun you with a long list of laws, but understand nothing of the case in hand. They have theories of all kinds, but some one else must put them into practice.

I have seen a friend of mine in my own house make sport of one of these fellows. He counterfeited a kind of nonsensical tongue made up of disjointed bits, without head or tail, except that once in a while he interjected some term relative to the dispute. Would you believe it, the blockhead was played upon the whole afternoon, all the while thinking he had answered pertinently and learnedly all objec-

A pedant ridiculed.

tions? And yet this fellow was a man of letters and reputation, and a fine gentleman of the long gown.

"Vos O patricius sanguis, quos vivere fas est
Occipiti cæco posticæ occurrite sannæ." [113]

("But you, patrician youths! whose skulls are blind,
Watch well your jeering friends, and look behind.")

Whoever will pry into and thoroughly sift these people, as I have done, will find, for the most part, they neither understand others nor themselves.

Pedants have little judgment.

Their memories are good enough, but the judgment is totally void and empty. The exceptions are those whose own nature has of itself formed them into something better. For example, Adrian Turnebus, who never made any other profession except that of letters, had nothing at all in him of the pedant. In my opinion, he was the most learned man this last thousand years has produced; still the only thing by which he was distinguished from ordinary men was the wearing of his gown and a little oddity of manner—which amounts to nothing. I hate those people who are more annoyed by an ill-fitting robe than by an ill-fashioned mind, and will pretend to tell what sort of man one is by his bow, by his behaviour, even by the shape of his boots. There was not a more refined and polished soul upon earth. I often purposely brought up questions quite wide of his profession, and found he had so clear an insight, so quick an apprehension, and so solid a judgment, you would think he had been a soldier, or had been employed in affairs of state all his life. These are great and vigorous natures—

> "Queis arte benigna,
> Et meliore luto finxit præcordia Titan,"[114]

("Formed of superior clay,
And animated by a purer ray,")

and can keep themselves upright in spite of a pedantic education. But it is not enough that our education does not spoil us, it must change us for the better. Some of our parliaments and courts admit officers after testing them as to their learning; others, in addition, require their judgment in some case of law. The second method is the better, I think. Both are necessary, and it is very essential that men should be defective in neither; yet knowledge is not so absolutely necessary as judgment. The latter may get along without the former, never without the latter. For as the Greek verse says, "'Ως οὐδὲν ἡ μάθησις ἢν μὴ νοῦς παρῇ;"[115]

("To what use serves learning if the understanding be away?") Would to God, for the sake of justice, our courts were as well furnished with understanding and conscience as they are with knowledge! "Non vitæ, sed scholæ discimus."[116] ("We learn not for life, but for the school.") We are not to tie learning to the mind, but work them together; not to tinge the mind only, but to give it a thorough and perfect dye. If it will not take colour and improve its imperfect state, it is much better to leave it alone. A sword is a dangerous weapon, and very likely to wound its master, if put into an awkward and unskilful hand. "Ut fuerit melius non didicisse."[117] ("So it were better never to have learned at all.")

And this, perhaps, is the reason why neither we nor the Christian religion require much learning in women. Francis, Duke of Brittany, son of John the Fifth, who married Isabella of Scotland, was once told that his wife was homely bred and without any manner of learning. Francis replied that he loved her all the better.[118] So it is no great wonder that our ancestors had but little use for letters; and, even at the present day, we rarely find a literary man in the councils of our princes. If we did not wish

Women require little learning.

to become rich—the chief object of life at the present time—by means of law, medicine, teaching, and even divinity itself, learning and letters would be as disregarded as ever. And would there be any loss either, since they neither instruct us to think well nor to do well? "Postquam docti prodierunt, boni desunt."[119] ("After once they become learned, they cease to be good.") All other learning is hurtful to him who has not the knowledge of honesty and goodness.

But may not the reason for this condition of affairs be found in the fact, as I have just stated, that our studies in France aim at profit? Some seem better fitted by nature for employments of glory than of gain. These, however, are taken from their studies before they have any taste for them and put at a profession which has nothing to do with books. None are left to apply themselves wholly to learning but people of mean condition, born to base fortune, who hope to earn a living thereby. The minds of such people are, by nature, education, and home example, of the basest metal; the fruits of knowledge are immaturely gathered, and badly digested. It is not the proper business of knowledge to enlighten the mind

Some more fit for business than the pursuit of knowledge.

that is dark of itself—not to make the blind see. Her business is not to furnish a man eyes, but to guide, govern, and direct his steps, provided he has sound feet and straight, capable legs. Knowledge is an excellent drug, but no drug has virtue enough to preserve itself from corruption and decay if the vessel in which it is kept be tainted and impure. Some on account of a squint see what is good but do not follow it, and perceive knowledge but make no use of it. Plato in his Republic lays down as his principal rule that his citizens should be fitted with employments suited to their natures. Nature can do all, and does all. Cripples are unfit for exercises of the body, and lame souls for exercises of the mind. Degenerate and vulgar minds are unworthy of philosophy. If we see a shoemaker out at the toes, we say, "It is no wonder; for commonly none go worse shod than they." The same way, experience has often shown us physicians less healthy than other people.

Aristo of Chios had reason to say that philosophers harmed their listeners because *People may apply* most of those who heard were *learning to evil* not capable of getting any benefit from their instruction, and if they did not apply what they learned to good, would certainly apply it to evil. "ἀσώτους ex Aristippi, acerbos ex Zenonis schola exire."[120] ("They came from the school of Aristippus debauchees, from the school of Zeno sour churls.")

In that education which Xenophon attributes to the Persians, we find they taught their children virtue as other nations do letters. Plato tells us how the eldest son in their royal succession was brought up. As soon as he was born he was delivered, not to women, but to eunuchs of the greatest authority and virtue, who were to keep his body in good shape and in health, and after he was seven years of age to teach him to ride and hunt. At fourteen, he was given into the hands of four men, the most noted in the kingdom for wisdom, justice, temperance, and valour. The first was to instruct him in religion, the second that he should be always upright and sincere, the third how to subdue his appetites and desires, and the fourth to despise all danger. It is worthy of notice that in the excellent and, as I may term it, matchless policy of Lycurgus, little mention is made of learning, even in the very seat of the Muses, though he was extremely careful of the education of children. Thus it would appear that their generous youths disdained all subjec-

Persian system of education.

OF PEDANTRY.

tion except that of virtue, and were supplied, instead of with tutors in the arts and sciences, with such masters only as should instruct them in valour, prudence, and justice; an example which Plato followed in his laws. Their manner of teaching was to propose questions, training the boys to judge of men and their actions. In this way the understanding was sharpened, and they learned what was right and lawful; for if they praised or condemned this or that person, or fact, they were to give a reason for so doing.

Xenophon tells us that Astyages once asked Cyrus to give an account of his last lesson, and received this answer: "A great boy in the school, having a short coat, by force took a longer from another who was not so tall as he, and gave his own in exchange. I was appointed judge of the controversy, and decided that each should keep the coat he had, for they were both better fitted now than they were before. Upon which my master told me I had done wrong, in that I only considered the fitness of the garment, whereas I should have considered the justice of the thing, which required that no one should have anything which is his own forcibly taken from him."[121] Cyrus added that he was

Cyrus whipped for an unjust decision.

whipped for his pains, as we are in our villages for forgetting the first aorist of τύπτω. My pedant must make me a very long oration, indeed, *in genere demonstrativo*, before he can persuade me his school is as good as that. They went to work in the shortest way, and seeing that the sciences when properly understood and rightly applied can not fail to teach us prudence, honesty, and integrity, they thought best to initiate their children at once in the knowledge of cause and effect, and to instruct them not by hearsay and rote, but by experiment and action; forming and moulding them not only by words and precepts, but principally by deeds and examples. In this way knowledge is not only in the mind, but is a complexion and habit; not an acquisition, but a natural possession. Agesilaus was once asked what he thought most proper for boys to learn? "What they ought to do when they come to be men."[122] It is no wonder that such an education produced admirable effects.

They used to go, it is said, to the other cities of Greece for rhetoricians, painters, and musicians, but to Lacedemon for legislators, magistrates, and generals of armies. At Athens they learned to speak well, here to do well; there to disengage themselves from a sophistical argument and to unravel ensnaring syllogisms; here to evade the baits and allurements of pleasure, and with noble courage and resolution to conquer the menaces of fortune and death.

<small>Athenian and Spartan systems of education contrasted.</small>

The Athenians bothered their brains about words, the Spartans made it their business to inquire into things; in the one city there was a continual babble of the tongue, in the other a constant exercise of the mind. And it is not strange, therefore, that when Antipater demanded of the Spartans fifty children for hostages, they answered, quite contrary to what we should do, that they would rather give him twice as many full-grown men, so much did they value their country's education. Agesilaus invited Xenophon to send his children to Sparta to be educated. "Not to learn logic or rhetoric," he said, "but to be instructed in the noblest of all knowledge, namely, how to obey and how to command."[123] It is pleasant to see Socrates, after his blunt manner, rallying Hippias, who recounts to him what great sums of money he had gotten, especially in certain little villages of Sicily, by keeping school, while he received never a penny at Sparta. "What a stupid and foolish people they must be," said Socrates, "without sense or understanding, who make no account of grammar or poetry, and busy themselves in studying the genealogies and successions of their kings, the foundation, rise, and fall of states, and such old wives' tales."[124] After this, he made Hippias acknowledge their excellent form of public administration, the happiness and virtue of their private life, and left him to guess at the conclusion he made of the uselessness of his pedantic arts.

Examples have demonstrated for us that, both in military governments, and all others of a like active nature, the study of letters does more to weaken and enervate the courage of men than to fortify and incite it. The most powerful nation in the whole world at the present time is that of the Turks, a people equally remarkable for their estimation of arms and their contempt of letters. Rome was most valiant when she was least learned. The most warlike nations of our day are the most ignorant, of which the Scythians, Parthians, and the great Tamerlane are proof. When the Goths overran Greece, the only thing that preserved the libraries from fire was that some one ventured the opinion that the conquerors would do well to leave such trash to the Greeks, since

The least learned nations the most warlike.

it would divert them from the exercise of arms and fix them in a lazy and sedentary life.[125] When our King Charles VIII, almost without striking a blow, saw himself in possession of the kingdom of Naples and a considerable part of Tuscany, the nobility about him attributed this unexpected ease of conquest to the fact that the princes of Italy studied more to render themselves ingenious and learned than vigorous and warlike.

OF THE AFFECTION OF FATHERS TO THEIR CHILDREN.

To Madame D'Estissac. 126

Book II. Chapter VIII.

MADAM, if the strangeness and novelty of my subject, which generally give value to things, do not save me, I shall never come off with honour from this foolish attempt. Perhaps the oddity of the subject may make it pass. It is a strange fancy and one opposed to me naturally, caused by the thoughtful solitude into which for some years I have retired, that put into my head the foolish idea of writing. I find myself unprovided with other matters and present myself to myself for argument and subject. This is the only book in the world of its kind and is remarkable for nothing but its extravagance. Indeed, the subject is so frivolous that the best workman in the world could not give it a form worthy of esteem.

Montaigne considers his subject unique.

OF THE AFFECTION OF FATHERS. 111

Now, madam, as I am about to draw my own picture true to life, I shall be omitting an important feature did I fail to represent in it the honour I have ever paid to your merits. I mention this expressly at the head of this chapter, for the reason that, among your other good qualities, the love you have shown to your children holds one of the chief places. I remember at what age your husband left you a widow; the great and honourable matches you have refused; the firmness with which you have attended to your affairs, difficult though they were; the success with which you have managed all these is an evidence that we have not a more striking example of natural affection than yours.

Madame D'Estissac extolled as a good mother.

I praise God, madam, that your efforts have been so well employed. The great promise that Monsieur D'Estissac, your son, gives of himself is sufficient assurance that when he comes of age you will receive the obedience and gratitude of a good man. On account of his tender years, he has not been capable of noticing these numberless acts of kindness which he has received from you. I shall therefore take care, if these papers ever fall into his hands, that he receives from

Gratitude due her from her son.

me this testimony. As a result of your kindness, he will see and feel that there is not a gentleman in France who stands more indebted to a mother's care than he does. He can then give proof of his own worth and virtue, by acknowledging you for that excellent mother you are.

If there can be any natural law, or instinct, which holds good universally, in my opinion, the first is self-preservation, while the affection which the parent bears to his offspring holds the second place. Nature seems to have recommended this to us, having regard for the extension and progression of the race. On the contrary, it is no wonder the regard of children toward their parents is not so great. To this we may add the other Aristotelian consideration, that he who confers a benefit loves better than he is beloved again, and he to whom a debt is due better than he from whom it is due.[127] Every artificer cares more for his work than the work would for the artificer if it had sense. We delight to be, and to be consists in moving and acting; in this way every one has, in some sort, a being in his work. Whoever confers a benefit exercises a fine and honourable action; he who receives it exercises the *utile*

Parental affection is greater than filial.

only. Now the *utile* is much less lovable than the *honestum* (the honourable), which is stable and permanent, supplying him who has done it with a continual gratification. The *utile* loses itself, easily glides away, and the memory of it is neither so fresh nor so pleasing. Those things are dearest to us which have cost us most, and giving is more enjoyable than receiving.

Since it has pleased God to endow us with some capacity for weighing things, we ought sometimes to yield to the simple authority of nature, as do the brutes, but not allow ourselves to be tyrannized over. Reason alone should have control of our inclinations. I, for my part, have a strange dislike for those inclinations that are started in us without the direction of the judgment. In this connection, I dislike that habit of dandling and caressing infants too young to render themselves lovable, having neither motion of soul nor shape of body, and I have not allowed them to be nursed near me.[128] A true and well-regulated affection ought to spring up and increase with the knowledge they give us of themselves. And then if they are worthy of it, natural feeling, going hand in hand with reason, should cherish them with a truly pa-

Children's rights.

ternal love. Most commonly, however, we find ourselves more interested in the first trotting about, the little ways and plays of our children, than we are afterward with their formed actions. It is as if we loved them for our sport, like monkeys, and not as men. There are some, too, very liberal in buying them playthings when they are children who are very close-handed for the least necessary expense when they grow up; so much so, that it looks as if we were jealous of seeing them appear in the world when we are about to leave it. It annoys us to have them tread upon our heels as if to urge us to leave. For my part, I think it cruelty and injustice not to receive them into a share of our goods. When they are capable, they should be informed of our domestic affairs, and we should lessen our own expenditures to leave more for theirs. It is unjust that an old fellow, deaf, lame, and half-dead, should alone in the chimney-corner enjoy the goods that are sufficient for many children, and allow them in the meantime to lose their best years for want of means to put themselves forward in the public service. A man in this way may drive his children to desperate measures and to seek out any means, no matter how dishonest, to provide for their own support. . . .

OF THE AFFECTION OF FATHERS.

A lord of very good understanding once told me that he hoarded up wealth, not to derive any use from it himself, but to make himself honoured and sought after by his relatives. When age should deprive him of other powers, it was the only remaining means to maintain his authority in his family, and to keep him from being neglected and despised by all the world. In fact, not only old age but every other infirmity, according to Aristotle,[129] is a promoter of avarice. A father is very miserable who has no other hold on his children's affections than the need they have of his assistance. He must render himself worthy of respect by his virtue and wisdom, and beloved by the bounty and the sweetness of his manners. Even the ashes of rich matter have value, and we generally, by custom, hold the bones of worthy men in reverence. No old age can be offensive in a man who has passed his life in honour; it must be venerable, especially to his children whom he has trained up to their duty by reason, not by roughness and force and the need they have of him.

A father should be respected for himself, not for his money.

" Et errat longe, mea quidem sententia,
  Qui imperium credat esse gravius aut stabilius
  Vi quod fit, quam illud quod amicitia adjungitur." [130]

("And he extremely differs from my sense,
Who thinks the power obtained by violence
Can ever prove more solid and secure
Than that which friendship's softer means procure.")

I condemn all violence in the education [131] of a gentle soul that is designed for honour and liberty. I am of the opinion that what can not be done by reason, prudence, and tact is never to be effected by force. I myself was brought up in this way; they tell me I never felt the rod but twice, and then very slightly. I have followed the same method with my children, all of whom died very young except Leonora, my only daughter.[132] She escaped that misfortune and has come to more than six years of age without other correction than words, and those very gentle. And though my expectations be frustrated, there are other causes on which to lay the fault without blaming my discipline, which I know to be natural and just. I should have been even more scrupulous toward sons as born to less subjection. I should have delighted to swell their hearts with ingenuousness and freedom. I have never observed other effects of whipping than to render children more cowardly or more wilful and obstinate. Do we wish to be beloved of our children, would we

Physical violence condemned.

OF THE AFFECTION OF FATHERS. 117

remove from them all occasion of wishing our death, though "Nullum scelus rationem habet"[131] ("No crime can have a justification"), let us reasonably satisfy their lives with what is in our power. In order to do this, we should not marry so young that our age shall in a measure be confounded with theirs. I speak more especially of the gentry, who live, as the phrase is, upon their income. In other conditions, where life is dedicated to making money, a large number of children is an advantage, being so many tools wherewith to grow rich. . . .

Parents and children should be friends. I have always thought it must be a great satisfaction to an aged father to put his children in the way of attending to his affairs; to have the power during his lifetime of guiding their behaviour, giving them instruction and advice from his own experience, and himself to transfer the ancient honour and order of his house into the hands of those who are to succeed him. In order to do this, I would not avoid their company. I would have them near at hand, and partake, according to the condition of my age, of their feasts and amusements. . . . I would endeavour by a sweet and obliging disposition to create in my children a lively and unfeigned friendship and good-will, a thing not hard to do in well-born natures. Of course, if they be brutes—and our age produces thousands—we must hate and avoid them as such. I am angry at the custom which forbids children to call their father by the name of father and enforces another title as more full of respect and reverence, as if nature had not sufficiently provided for our authority. We call God father, and refuse to have our children call us so. I have reformed this error in my family. It is also folly and injustice to deprive them, when grown up, of a familiarity with their father, and to carry an austere countenance toward them, thinking to keep them in awe and obedience. They possess youth and vigour and consequently the breath and favour of the world. They receive these fierce and tyrannical looks (mere scarecrows) of a man without blood either in his heart or veins with mockery and contempt. Though I could make myself feared, I would much rather make myself beloved. . . .

The late Marshal de Montluc lost his son in the island of Madeira.[134] He was a very brave young man, and much was expected of him by his father, who confessed to me, among other regrets, what a sorrow and heart-breaking it was that he had never made himself familiarly acquainted with his son. An extreme fatherly gravity had prevented him from knowing his son, as well as of showing his great affection and the high opinion he had of his noble nature. "The poor boy," said he, "never saw in me other than a stern, forbidding countenance, and is gone in a belief that I neither knew how to love nor esteem him according to his desert. For whom did I reserve the wonderful affection I had in my soul? Was it not he himself who should have had all the pleasure of it? I forced myself to put on and maintain this vain disguise, and have by that means deprived myself of the pleasure of his companionship, and in some measure of his affection, which could not be warm toward me, he having never seen me other than austere." Marshal de Montluc had reason for this complaint, I know. As for myself, a certain experience [135] has taught me that in the loss of friends there is no consolation so sweet as the consciousness of having had no reserve with them, but a perfect and entire familiarity. . . .

Mistake of the Marshal de Montluc.

I open myself to my family as much as I can, and very willingly let them know my opinion and good-will toward them, as I do to everybody else. I allow them to know me thoroughly, for I would not have them mistaken in me in anything. Among other curious customs of the Gauls, Cæsar [136] reports that the sons never presented themselves before their father nor dared appear in his company until they began to bear arms. This would seem to indicate that the father was then ready to receive them into his acquaintance and friendship.

Children should be somewhat familiar with their parents.

OF LIARS.

Book I, Chapter IX.

In truth, lying is a hateful and accursed vice. When we lie we are not men, for we have no other tie upon one another than our word. If we only could know the horror and bad consequence of it, we should pursue it with fire and sword, and more justly than any other crime. —I notice that parents, with great indiscretion, correct their children for little innocent faults, and torment them for childish tricks that make no impression and have no bad results. On the other hand, lying and wilful obstinacy are the faults which ought on all occasions to be repressed, or they will grow and develop with the child. After the tongue has once caught the knack of lying, it is almost impossible to eradicate it. For this reason we see some who are otherwise very good men subject to this fault. I have for my tailor an honest fellow whom I have never found guilty of

Children should be trained to speak the truth.

a single truth—no, not even when it would have been to his advantage. If falsehood had like truth but one face we should get on better, for we should then take the contrary of what the liar says for certain truth. But the reverse of truth has a hundred thousand shapes, and is a field without bound or limit. The Pythagoreans made good to be certain and finite [definite]; evil infinite [indefinite] and uncertain.[137]

Also Book II, Chapter XVIII.

The first feature in the corruption of manners is the banishment of truth; for, as Pindar says, to be true is the beginning of a great virtue, and it is the first qualification that Plato requires in the governor of his republic. In these days the truth is not so much what it really is, but what every man persuades others; just as we give the name of money not only to good pieces but to the false also, if they are current and will pass. Our nation has long been reproached with this fault. Salvianus Massiliensis, who lived in the time of Valentinianus, says, "Lying and perjury are not vices with the French, but a way of speaking." Any one coming upon this testimony might say it is now a virtue with them. Men edu-

Falsehood the beginning of corruption.

cate themselves to it as an exercise of honour, for dissimulation is one of the most notable qualities of this age. . . .

Lying is a base, unworthy vice—a vice that one of the ancients [138] portrays in most odious colours when he says, that it is to manifest a contempt of God and a fear of men. It is not possible to show more clearly the horror, baseness, and irregularity of it. Who can imagine anything more contemptible than for a man to be a coward toward men and valiant against his Maker? Intelligence is conveyed by speaking, and he who falsifies betrays public society. It is only by speech that we can communicate our thoughts and wills; it is the interpreter of the soul, if it be misleading, we no longer are certain nor have any hold upon one another. If speech deceive us, it destroys all our intercourse and dissolves all ties of government.

A lie is contemptible.

OF HABIT.

Book I, Chapter XXII.

PLATO once reproved a boy for playing at nuts. "You reprove me," said the boy, "for a little thing." "Habit," replied Plato, "is not a little thing."[139]

Plato on habit.

Our greatest vices have their beginnings in tender infancy; our principal education depends upon the nurse. Mothers are greatly amused to see a child twist off the neck of a chicken, or entertain himself with tormenting a dog or a cat.[140] And there is many a wise father, too, who considers it a sign of martial spirit when he hears his son domineer over a poor peasant or lackey that dares not answer back. The father considers it a great sign of brains when he sees his boy cheat and overreach his play-fellows by some sly trick. And yet these are the true seeds and roots of cruelty, tyranny, and treason. They bud in childhood, and afterward shoot up vigorously in the field of habit,

Parents to blame for not correcting childish vices.

and it is a very dangerous mistake to excuse these evil inclinations because of the child's tender age or the triviality of the subject. First, it is Nature that is speaking when her voice is more sincere and her thoughts less disguised, being younger and more active. Secondly, the deformity of cheating does not depend upon the difference between crowns and pins, but entirely upon itself; for a cheat is a cheat, be it small or great. This leads me to think it more just to conclude, "why should he not cheat in crowns since he cheats in pins?" than as they say, "he plays only for pins, he would not do it if it were for crowns." Children should be carefully taught to abhor vices for themselves, and the hideousness of these vices ought to be so represented that they may avoid them not only in their actions, but abominate them from their hearts, so that the very thought will be hateful to them, however masked the vices may be.

I know this to be true from my own experience. I was brought up to a plain and sincere manner of dealing, and had an aversion to all kinds of juggling and dishonesty in my childish sports and recreations. And it should be noted here that the play of children is

Plays of children of great importance.

not really play, but must be judged as their most serious actions.[141] There is no game, however small, in which naturally and without study and endeavour I have not an extreme aversion to deceit. I shuffle and cut and make as much ado with the cards, keeping as strict account of my farthings as I would for doubloons. When winning or losing against my wife and daughter, it is the same as when I play in good earnest with others for round sums. At all times and in all things my own eyes are sufficient to watch my fingers. No one watches me so closely, nor is there any one I more fear to offend than myself.

OF PRESUMPTION.

Book II, Chapter XVII.

I AGAIN fall to talking of the vanity of our education, the end of which is not to make us good and wise, but learned. Education has not taught us to follow and embrace virtue and prudence, but she has imprinted in us their derivation and etymology. We know how to decline the word virtue, even if we know not how to love it. If we do not know what prudence really is, in effect and by experience, we at least have the etymology and meaning of the word by heart. We are not content to know the extraction, kindred, and alliances of our neighbours, we would have them for our friends. This education of ours has taught us the definitions, divisions, and partitions of virtue as so many surnames and branches of a genealogy, without any care to establish an intimacy between us and her. Education, for our initiatory instruction, has chosen not

Formal education condemned.

such books as contain the soundest and truest opinions, but such as speak the best Greek and Latin, and by fine words has filled our minds with the vainest notions of antiquity. . . .

There is no soul so coarse and wretched wherein some particular faculty may not be found; no soul so buried in sloth that it may not be awakened in some way. How it happens that a man blind and asleep may be found bright, clear, and excellent in some one thing, we are to inquire of our masters. But the beautiful souls are those that are universal, open and ready for all things, if not taught, at least capable of being taught. . . .

<small>Everyone susceptible to instruction.</small>

A good education alters the judgment and the manners, as in the case of Polemon,[142] a young debauched Greek, who going by chance to hear one of Xenocrates' lectures, not only observed the eloquence and learning of the professor and brought away some important knowledge, but, what was better, suddenly changed and reformed his manner of life. Did any one ever hear of such an effect from our teaching? . . .

<small>Education reformatory.</small>

I find the manners and language of country people commonly better suited to the rule of true philosophy than those of our philosophers themselves. "Plus sapit vulgus, quia tantum, quantum opus est sapit." [143] ("The vulgar are so much wiser because they know only what is needful for them to know.")

Vernacular suited to philosophy.

OF PHYSIOGNOMY.

Book III, Chapter XII.

It has happened well that the man most worthy to be known, and to be presented to the world as an example, is the one of whom we have the most certain knowledge. Socrates has been revealed to us by the most clear-sighted men that ever lived, and their testimonies are admirable both in matter and fidelity. It is a great thing that Socrates so understood the pure imagination of a child, that he was able, without twisting or changing it, to produce a most beautiful effect in the human soul. He shows the soul neither elevated nor rich; he only represents it sound, but with a pure and vigorous health. By natural means, by ordinary and common fancies,[144] he presented not only the most regular, but the highest and most vigorous beliefs, actions, and manners that ever existed. It was he who brought from heaven, where she was losing her time, human wisdom, to restore her to man,

Simplicity commended.

with whom her great business most truly lies. See him plead before his judges; notice by what reasons he arouses his courage to the fortunes of war; with what arguments he fortifies his patience against calumny, tyranny, death, and the shrewishness of his wife. You will find nothing in all this borrowed from the arts and sciences. The simplest may here discover their own means and power. It is not possible to be more humble. He has done human nature a kindness by showing it how much it can do of itself.

All of us are richer than we think, but we are taught to borrow and to beg, and are brought up to make more use of what is another's than of our own. Man is unable to conform himself to his mere necessity. Of everything—pleasure, wealth, and power—he grasps more than he can hold. His greediness is incapable of moderation. I find, too, in desire for knowledge, he is the same. He cuts out more work than he can do, and more than he needs to do, extending the utility of knowledge to its matter. "Ut omnium rerum sic litterarum quoque intemperantia laboramus."[145] ("As of everything else we are also afflicted with intemperance in letters.") Tacitus has reason to commend the

Intemperance in letters.

mother of Agricola for restraining her son in his violent appetite for learning.[146]

<small>Little learning needed to live well.</small> That is desirable, if duly considered, which has in it, like the other possessions of man, a great deal of vanity, a proper and natural weakness, and costs very dear. The acquisition of learning is more hazardous than that of meat or drink. Other things that we buy we can carry home in a vessel, and there examine our purchase, and decide when and how much of it we will take. From the very first, we put our knowledge into no vessel but the soul. We swallow it as we buy it, and return from the market already injured or benefited. Some things only burden and overcharge the stomach instead of nourishing; and others, under the pretence of curing, poison us. I have been pleased in places where I have travelled to see men out of devotion make a vow of ignorance as well as of chastity, poverty, and penitence. It is also a checking of our unruly appetites to blunt this cupidity that spurs us on to the study of books, and to deprive the soul of this voluptuous complacency that tickles us with the idea of knowledge. It is fully to carry out the vow of poverty to add unto it that of the mind. We need little learning to show

us how to live at ease. Socrates tells us that it is in us, how we may find it and how to use it. All knowledge that exceeds the natural is well-nigh superfluous. It is more likely to burden us than do us good. "Paucis opus est litteris ad mentem bonam."[147] ("A man of good natural parts needs little learning.") It is a feverish excess of the mind, a tempestuous and unquiet instrument. Collect yourself; you will find in your own mind the arguments of nature against death and those best suited to serve you in time of need. It is these arguments that make a peasant, an entire people, die with as much firmness as a philosopher.

OF ANGER.

Book II, Chapter XXXI.

Children should be educated by the state.

In nothing is Plutarch more happy than when he judges of human actions. Especially is this true in his parallel of Lycurgus and Numa, in which he speaks of the folly of abandoning children to the care and direction of their fathers. As Aristotle says, most of our civil governments, after the manner of the Cyclops, leave to every one the ordering of wife and children according to his own foolish and indiscreet fancy.[148] The Lacedæmonians and Cretans are almost the only governments that have committed the education of children to the laws. And yet who does not see that in a state all depends upon their nurture and bringing up? They are, however, left to the mercy of parents, no matter how foolish and wicked they may be.

As I pass along the street I have often

thought of writing a comedy to avenge the poor boys whom I have seen flogged, knocked down, and miserably beaten by some father or mother mad with rage. You see parents come out with fire and fury sparkling in their eyes, and with a roaring, terrible voice;

Parents in punishing their children often injure them.

> "Rabie jecur incendente feruntur
> Præcipites; ut saxa jugis abrupta, quibus mons
> Subtrahitur, clivoque latus pendente recedit." [149]

> ("As when impetuous winds and driving rain
> Have mined a rock that overhung the plain,
> The massy ruin falls with thundering force,
> And bears all down that interrupts its course.")

The most dangerous maladies, says Hippocrates, are those that disfigure the countenance. Those who are just from the nurse are often treated in this way and are lamed and injured by blows, while our justice takes no notice of it, as if these maims and dislocations were not inflicted upon members of our commonwealth.

> "Gratum est, quod patriæ civem populoque dedisti,
> Si facis, ut patriæ sit idoneus, utilis agris,
> Utilis et bellorum et pacis rebus agendis." [150]

> ("True, you have given a citizen to Rome,
> And she shall thank you if the youth become,
> By your o'erruling care, or soon or late,
> An useful member of the parent state;

Fit to assist the earth in her increase,
And proper for affairs of war and peace.")

There is no passion that so turns men from their right judgment as anger. No one would demur at punishing with death a judge who should condemn a criminal on account of his own wrath. Why, then, should parents and teachers be allowed to whip children in their anger? It is then no longer correction, but revenge. Punishment is instead of medicine to children; and would we tolerate a physician who was enraged at his patient? We ourselves would do well never to lay a hand upon our servants while angry. Let us defer the business so long as the pulse beats quick. Things will appear otherwise when we are calm and cool. In anger, it is passion that commands and speaks, not we. Faults seen through passion are magnified and appear much greater to us than they really are, like bodies seen through a mist. He who is hungry uses meat, but he who would make use of correction should have no appetite either of hunger or thirst to it. Besides, punishments that are inflicted with deliberation and discretion are much better received and with greater benefit by him who suffers. Otherwise, he will think himself unjustly condemned by a

Anger perverts justice.

man beside himself with anger, and will bring forward the judge's excessive passion, his inflamed countenance, his oaths, his strange actions, for his own justification.

> "Ora tument ira, nigrescunt sanguine venæ,
> Lumina Gorgoneo sævius igne micant."[151]

> ("Rage swells the lips, with black blood fill the veins,
> And in their eyes fire worse than Gorgon's reigns."

Suetonius reports that Caius Rabirius having been condemned by Cæsar appealed to the people, who determined the cause in his favour because of the animosity and harshness Cæsar had shown in the sentence.[152]

THE ART OF CONVERSATION.

Book III, Chapter VIII.

Who has ever gained wisdom by his logic? "Nec ad melius vivendum, nec ad commodius disserendum."[153] ("It neither makes a man live better nor reason more aptly.") Is there more noise or confusion in the scolding of fishwives than in the public disputations of scholars? I would rather have my son learn to speak in a tavern than to prate in the schools of rhetoric. Take a master of arts, converse with him; why does not he convince us of his artificial excellence? Why does he not enchant women and ignorant fellows like us with admiration at the steadiness of his reasons and the beauty of his order? Why does he not persuade and sway us at will? Why does a man who has so great advantage in matter, mingle railing, indiscretion, and fury, in his disputation? Strip him of his gown, his hood,

Learning does not teach effective expression.

and his Latin, and you would take him for one of us, or worse. While they torment us with this confusion of words, it fares with them, I think, as with jugglers; their dexterity deceives our senses, but does not change our belief. Out of this legerdemain they perform nothing that is not very ordinary. Being learned they are not the less fools.

I love and honour knowledge as much as those who have it, and used properly it is the most noble and the most powerful acquisition of men. But men such as I speak of—and their number is infinite—place their fundamental reliance upon it, and appeal from their understanding to their memory, "sub aliena umbra latentes"[154] ("hiding under borrowed shade"), and can do nothing except by book. I hate it, if I may dare say so, even worse than stupidity itself. In my country, and in my time, learning improves many fortunes but not minds. If it comes in contact with those that are dull and heavy, it overcharges and suffocates them, leaving them with a crude and undigested mass. If the mind is airy and fine, it purifies, clarifies, and subtilizes them to inanition. Learning thus becomes a thing of varying quality, a very useful accession to a well-

Knowledge useless which does not improve the mind.

born soul, but hurtful and pernicious to others.[155] It is rather a very precious thing that will not suffer itself to be purchased under value. In the hands of some it is a sceptre, in the hands of others a fool's bauble.

OF IDLENESS.

Book I, Chapter VIII.

WE see ground that has long remained fallow, and grown rich and fertile by rest, abound with innumerable weeds and unprofitable wild herbs. To make it perform its true functions, we must cultivate and prepare it for such seed as we consider proper. . . . So it is with our minds. If we do not apply them to some sort of study that will fix and restrain them, they will drift into a thousand extravagances, and will sternly run here and there in an inextricable labyrinth of restless imagination. . . . In this wild and irregular agitation there is no folly nor idle fancy they do not touch upon:

Mind requires occupation.

> "Velut ægri somnia, vanæ
> Fingentur species." [156]

("Like sick men's dreams, that, from a troubled brain,
Phantasms create, ridiculous and vain.")

The soul that has no established limits to circumscribe it, loses itself. As the epigrammatist says, "He that is everywhere is nowhere."

"Quisquis ubique habitat,
 Maxime, nusquam habitat." [157]

OF EXPERIENCE.

Book III, Chapter XIII.

Go back to nature for wisdom.

PHILOSOPHERS, with good reason, send us back to the rules of nature, but they themselves have nothing to do with such sublime knowledge. They misrepresent and show us her face painted with too high and too sophisticated a colour, for which reason we have so many portraits of so uniform a subject. As philosophy has given us feet with which to walk, so she has given us prudence to guide us in life; not such an ingenious, robust, and majestic a prudence as that of their invention, but one that is easy, quiet, and healthful. It very well performs the promises to him who has the good fortune to know how to apply it sincerely and regularly—that is to say, according to nature. The more simply a man commits himself to nature, the more wisely. Oh, what soft, easy, and wholesome pillows are ignorance and indifference whereon to lay a well-made head! I would rather understand myself well in myself than in Cicero. I have had enough experience to make me wise, if I were only a good scholar. Any one who will recall an instance of anger, and who remembers the fever that transformed him, will realize the deformity better than in Aristotle, and will conceive a more just hatred of it. Whoever will remember the dangers he has escaped, those that threaten him, and the slight occasions that have removed him from one condition to another, will by that means prepare himself for future changes, and give him a knowledge of his state. The life of Cæsar himself is no greater example than our own; both popular and imperial, it is still a life to which all human accidents may refer. . . .

In my childhood what they had to correct me for most often was my refusal of those things which children commonly love best, such as sugar and sweetmeats. My tutor contended with this aversion to delicacies as a kind of over-nicety, and indeed it is nothing but a peculiarity of taste. Any one who should cure a child of an obstinate liking for brown bread, bacon, and garlic could cure him of all kinds of delicacy. . . . It is a sign of an effemi-

Children should be trained to like ordinary things.

nate nature to dislike ordinary and accustomed things. . . . It is better to train one's appetite to those things which are to be procured most easily, but it is always bad to pamper one's self. I once called effeminate a relative of mine who while in the galleys had learned not to use beds, and not to undress when he went to sleep.

If I had sons I should heartily wish them my fortune. The good father God gave me, Children should not be brought up in luxury. who had nothing of me but the acknowledgment of his bounty —a very hearty one—sent me from my cradle to live in a poor village of his. I remained there all the time I was being nursed, and even longer, and was brought up in the meanest and most common way of living; "Magna pars libertatis est bene moratus venter."[158] ("A well-regulated stomach is a great part of liberty.") Never take upon yourselves, much less leave to your wives, the bringing up of your children. Leave their shaping to fortune, under natural and human laws. Leave it to custom to train them up to frugality and austerity that they may rather rise from hardships than come to them. My father had also another idea, and that was to make me familiar with those people and that class of men which most need our assistance. He believed that I would have more regard for those who had helped me than for those who had not. For the same reason also he provided me with godfathers of the most humble condition. And his design succeeded, for I have a very kind inclination toward the meaner sort of people, whether it be out of condescension or out of natural compassion.

HISTORY.

Book II, Chapter X.

History best taught by biography.

THE historians, however, are my true men, for they are pleasant and easy, and in them I find man in general, the knowledge of whom I hunt after, more lively and entire than anywhere else. Here are shown the variety and truth of his internal qualities, as a whole and in piecemeal; the different means by which he is united and knit; and the accidents that threaten him. Now, those that write lives, because they insist more upon counsels than events, more upon what comes from within than upon what happens without, are most proper for my reading; therefore, above all others, Plutarch is the man for me. I am sorry we have not a dozen like Diogenes Laertius, or that his history was not more extended or more comprehensive, for I am as curious to know the lives and fortunes of these great instructors of the world as to know their different doctrines and opinions.

Plutarch.

Studying history in this way a man must tumble over without distinction all sorts of authors, new and old, French and foreign, in order to know the things they variously treat. Cæsar, in my opinion, particularly deserves to be studied, not for knowledge only, but for himself, since he is so far above the rest, Sallust included. In truth, I read this author with more respect and reverence than are usually allowed to human writings, and I consider that in his person, by his actions and miraculous greatness, and by the purity and inimitable polish of his language and style, he not only excels all other historians, as Cicero confesses, but Cicero himself as well. He speaks of his enemies with so much sincerity of judgment that, excepting his pestilent ambition and the false colours with which he strives to palliate his bad cause, there is no fault to be found in him. It is true he speaks too sparingly of himself, especially since he must have had a greater share in the execution of many things than he gives himself credit for, seeing they could not have been performed except under his personal supervision.

Cæsar.

I love historians, whether they be of the simple kind or of the higher order. The first make it their business to collect all that comes to their knowledge, and faithfully to record all things without choice or prejudice, mixing nothing of their own with it, but leaving us the task of discerning the truth. Such a one is honest. Froissart, who has proceeded in his undertaking with so frank a plainness that, having committed an error, he is not ashamed to confess and correct it in the place where the finger has been laid. He gives us even the rumours that were then spread abroad, and the different reports that were made to him. These things are the naked and unformed material of history, of which everyone may make his profit according to his understanding. On the other hand, the more excellent historians have judgment to pick out what is most worthy to be known, and of two accounts to choose that which is the more likely to be true. From the condition of princes and their dispositions, they imagine the counsels, and attribute to them words proper for the occasion. These historians have the right to assume the responsibility of regulating our belief, because of what they themselves believe; but certainly this privilege belongs to very few. As for the middle sort of historians—to which class most

Classes of historians. Froissart.

belong—they spoil all. They chew our meat for us. They take upon themselves to judge of history, and consequently to bias it to their own fancy. If the judgment lean to one side, a man can not help twisting his narrative.[139] These historians undertake to select things worthy to be known, and yet often conceal from us such words and such private actions as would greatly instruct us; they omit as incredible the things they do not understand, as well as the things they are unable to express in good French or Latin. Let them display their eloquence and judge according to their own ideas, but at the same time let them leave us something to judge of also, and neither alter nor disguise by their abridgments and selections anything of the real matter, but give it to us pure and entire.

As a general rule, in these modern times, historians are chosen from among the mediocre people simply because they are graceful writers, as if we were to learn language from them. These men pretending to nothing but babble, and being hired for no other end, prepare us an interesting report they have picked up at the street corners, and they care little for the truth of the matter. The only really good historians are those who have taken part in the affairs of

<small>An eye-witness the best historian.</small>

which they write, or at least have had to do with others of the same nature; such were almost all the Greek and Roman historians. For several eye-witnesses having written of the same subject, at a time when greatness and learning often met in the same person, if there happened to be an error, it must of necessity be a very slight one, and upon a very doubtful incident. What can one expect from a physician who writes of war, or from a mere scholar treating of the plans of rulers?

Also Book I, Chapter XVI.

In reading history—a subject on which everybody writes—I consider what kind of men are the authors. If they be persons who profess nothing but mere learning, I observe their style and note their language. If they be physicians, I am inclined to credit what they report of the temperature of the air, of the health and temperament of princes, of wounds and diseases. If they be lawyers, we learn from them concerning the controversies of right and wrong, the establishment of laws and civil government, and so on. If they be divines, we believe what they say about the affairs of the church, ecclesiastical censures, marriages, and dis-

Value of history relative to the author.

pensations. Courtiers are authority upon manners and ceremonies, soldiers upon the things that properly belong to their profession, especially upon the accounts of actions and enterprises in which they were personally engaged; while from ambassadors we are to learn of their negotiations, diplomatic discoveries, adroit manœuvres, and how such things are to be carried on.

Also Book I, Chapter XX.

<small>Clergymen and philosophers should not write history.</small>

I am sometimes in doubt whether a divine or a philosopher, men of such exact wisdom and tender conscience, ought to write history, for how can they stake their reputation upon a popular belief? How be responsible for the opinions of men they do not know, or state their conjectures of truth? Even of actions performed before their own eyes, especially if several persons took part, they would be unwilling to give evidence upon oath before a judge, nor do they know any man well enough to become surety for his intentions. For my part, I think it less dangerous to write of things past than present. In the former instance the writer is only to give an account of things everyone knows he must of necessity take upon trust.

NOTES.

1. Page 20. Montaigne's expression is *me fiert*. It is thought that Rousseau owes to this word his discovery of the motto of the Solar Family: "Tel fiert que ne tue pas" (see Rousseau's Confessions, Part i, Book iii). The word itself is from the Latin *ferio*.

2. P. 22. Diogenes Laertius, Chrysippus, vii.

3. P. 22. Diogenes Laertius, Epicurus, x.

4. P. 23. This is literally true. Montaigne quoted more and more as he grew older. The first edition of his Essays (Bordeaux, 1580) has very few quotations. These become more numerous in the edition of 1588. The great multitude of classical texts, which at times overload the page, date only from the posthumous edition of 1595. He had annotated his previous edition during the last years of his life, as an amusement of his idleness. This explains also in part the varying translations.

5. P. 24. See chapter on Moral Education in Spencer's Education, where the same thought is amplified.

6. P. 25. This idea is taken from Plato's Dialogue, Theages. A father comes to Socrates for advice concerning his son's education. The reply was the same that Montaigne has here given. Jowett, however, considers Theages spurious, and does not include it in his edition of 1892.

7. P. 25. Republic, iii. "They (the rulers) should observe what elements mingle in their offspring, for if the son of a golden or silver parent has an admixture of brass or iron, then nature orders a transposition of ranks."

8. P. 28. *Tête bien faite*, an expression created by Montaigne, which has remained a part of the French language. The edition of 1580 has, "Je voudrois aussi qu'on fut soigneus de luy choisir un conducteur qui eut plustost la teste bien faicte que bien pleine." Locke is still more careful, and would not have a tutor changed any more than a man would his wife (sec. 92). Rousseau gives the tutor entire charge of Émile for twenty-five years, sends him to the country, and isolates him from society (Rousseau's Émile, New York, 1893, p. 15 *et seq.*). Dr. Thomas Arnold was entirely of Montaigne's opinion. "And to this I find myself coming more and more. I care less and less for information, more and more for the pure exercise of the mind. . . . What I want is a man who is a Christian and a gentleman—an active man, and one who has common sense and understands boys. . . . I prefer activity of mind, and an interest in his work to high scholarship" (quoted by Dr. Fitch in Thomas and Matthew Arnold, New York, 1897, p. 69 *et seq.*).

9. P. 28. Cicero, De Natura Deorum., i, 5.

10. P. 30. A remarkable example of Herbartian apperception and co-ordination two hundred years before Herbart.

11. P. 30. Seneca, Epist., 33.

12. P. 31. Dante, Inferno, xi, 93. "Che non men che saver, dubbiar m'aggrata."

13. P. 31. Seneca, Epist., 33.

14. P. 33. From this and other statements it is evi-

dent that Montaigne would be in hearty sympathy with the Herbartian doctrines of apperception and interest. See further, Theodor Arndt: Montaigne's Ideen über Erziehung; eine Studie zur Geschichte der Pädagogik, Dresden, 1875.

15. P. 34. The Santa Rotunda is the temple of Agrippa at Rome, completed about 25 B. C.; also called the Pantheon. After Alaric and Genseric had plundered it, Emperor Phocas gave it to Pope Boniface IV, who changed it into a Christian Church without any important alterations. Montaigne speaks of it in his Journey into Italy as very beautiful because of its brilliant illumination. "It is covered," he says, "from top to bottom with moving lamps, which keep turning about all night long." Busts of many eminent persons adorn the interior, and the painters Raphael, Annibale Caracci, and Mengs are buried here.

16. P. 35. Montaigne was not fortunate in either mother or wife, and this opinion is the direct result of his own observation. At the same time it shows one of his most serious limitations. The French have suffered severely for their shortsightedness in this direction. A genuine, pure family life constitutes an inestimable moral factor in the education of a child. Montaigne was an indifferent husband; Locke lost his mother when young, and never had sister or wife; Rousseau sent his children to the foundling's home soon after birth. It was reserved for Luther, Pestalozzi, and Froebel to emphasize by precept and example the great significance of the family in the education of the young.

17. P. 35. Horace, Ode, iii, 2, 5.
18. P. 36. Cicero, Tusc. Quæs., ii, 15.
19. P. 36. To be read in connection with pp. 35,

36, 62, 64. Montaigne here suggests the hardening method. Locke from these suggestions makes out a very elaborate system (sec. 1–9) with the same purpose in view. Locke, however, goes to extremes which are absurd—as, for example, his advice that a child's shoes be made so thin that they may "leak and let in water whenever he comes near it." For the contrary view, see Spencer's Physical Education, where he calls the hardening process a "grievous delusion." Rousseau does not keep pace with Locke, but thinks, nevertheless, that in time children may be bathed in water at the point of freezing (p. 24). Little or no headdress should be worn at any time of the year (p. 91).

20. P. 37. Montaigne speaks further concerning good manners in Book i, chapter xiii. "Not every country only, but every city and every society has a certain form of good manners. In this respect there was care enough taken in my education, and I have lived in good company enough to know the formalities of our own nation, and am able to give lessons in it. I love to follow them, but not to be so completely enslaved to their observation that my whole life should be given up to them. . . . I have seen some people rude by being over-civil and troublesome in their courtesy." Locke, too, warns young people of this "mistaken civility," and gives careful directions for training children in good breeding (sec. 144–145).

21. P. 38. Seneca, Epist., 103.
22. P. 38. Cicero, De Offic., i, 41.
23. P. 39. Cicero, Acad., v, 3, 39.
24. P. 42. Propertius, iv, 3, 39.
25. P. 42. Anticipating our modern idea of teaching history by means of biography, Rousseau quotes

Montaigne and heartily agrees with him (p. 216). See further, the extract from Essay X, Book ii.

26. P. 43. Plutarch, On False Shame.

27. P. 43. Estienne de la Boëtie, who wrote a book on Voluntary Servitude. A complete edition of La Boëtie's works was published in Paris, 1846. A touching and beautiful picture of the feeling which existed between the two men is drawn in Book i, Essay 27.

28. P. 44. Plutarch, Apothegms.
29. P. 44. Plutarch, On Exile.
30. P. 47. Cicero, Tusc. Quæs., v, 3.
31. P. 47. Persius, iii, 69.
32. P. 48. Virgil, Æneid, iii, 459.
33. P. 49. Horace, Epist., i, 2, 40.
34. P. 49. Propertius, v, 1, 85.
35. P. 49. Anacreon, Ode xvii, 10.
36. P. 50. Diogenes Laertius, ii.
37. P. 50. Theodore Gaza was a famous teacher of languages during the middle of the fifteenth century, and became rector of the Academy of Ferrara. He aided much in reviving classical studies in Europe, and his Greek Grammar was considered an authority for many years. Montaigne in his condemnation of Gaza, seems to have in mind our modern principle—in learning a language, endeavor to associate as much real knowledge with the words as is possible.

38. P. 52. Plutarch, On Oracles which have Ceased.

39. P. 52. Juvenal, Satire, ix, 18.

40. P. 53. Montaigne here, no doubt, is thinking of the subtleties and intricacies of logic. These Scholastic terms had been brought into vogue by Peter Hispanus in the latter part of the thirteenth century. See Ueberweg's System of Logic and History of

Logical Teachings (third edition, Bonn, 1865, pp. 271-337).

41. P. 54. Hesiod, Ἔργα καὶ Ἡμέραι, v, 27.

42. P. 54. Heroines of Ariosto's Orlando Furioso.

43. P. 56. On a copy of the edition of 1588, which Montaigne corrected with his own hand, is found the following remarkable passage: "That the tutor in good time strangle him, if he be without witnesses," etc. (see M. Naigeon's edition). The change must have been made later, either by the essayist himself or by Mlle. de Gourney, his first editor.

44. P. 56. Plato, Republic, iv. "The intention was that in the case of the citizens generally, each individual should be put to the use for which nature intended him."

45. P. 56. Persius, iii, 23. Luther had the same thought when he observed: "It is difficult to teach old dogs new tricks, but we have the young ones." Froebel, as we know, makes much of the same idea, and we find it also at the basis of Herbartian courses of study.

46. P. 57. Montaigne evidently gives children credit for considerable reflective power. Locke makes much of reasoning with children. "They love to be treated as rational creatures sooner than is imagined" (sec. 81).

47. P. 58. Persius, v, 64.

48. P. 58. Diogenes Laertius, x.

49. P. 59. *Ibid*, iv.

50. P. 59. Hobbes said that if he had been at college as long as other people he should have been as great a blockhead as they.

51. P. 60. Plutarch, Symp.

52. P. 60. Horace, Epist., i, 1, 25.

53. P. 61. The great attention given to physical training during the past twenty years indicates the necessity for this advice. Beginning September, 1897, Yale freshmen are compelled to do two hours' work a week in the gymnasium under direction. This is one of the latest evidences of the recognition by high authority of the close relation between mind and body.

54. P. 62. This should be read in connection with pages 116, 136, 137. Montaigne's experience with the harshness of his time is corroborated by the testimony of others. Erasmus says that the whip, imprisonments, and fasts were the fundamental principles of the education he remembered. Rabelais gives his opinion of the colleges of his time in these words: "Think not, my sovereign lord, I would place your son in that low college they call Montagu. I would rather place him among the grave-diggers of Saint Innocent, so enormous is the cruelty and villainy I have known there. The galley-slaves are far better used among the Moors and Tartars—yea, the very dogs in your house—than the poor, wretched students in the aforesaid college" (Rabelais, Book i, 37). The colleges of France were improved after a king of France had himself enrolled among the boys of the College of Navarre (Arnstädt, François Rabelais, Leip., 1872). Locke had some unpleasant reminiscences of Westminster School, and would advise men "not to endanger their sons' innocence for the sake of a little Greek and Latin" (sec. 70). Not only were the schools excessively cruel, but they were reprehensible for the general immorality of the students. Lord Chesterfield seemed to think a boy could not live a virtuous life at school (see Letters). Even as late as 1624, Duke Albrecht, of Saxony, writing of the University of

Jena, complains of the innumerable disorders, excesses, blasphemies, looseness of words and actions, and in eating and drinking, and all manner of vicious and godless actions, sometimes extending to murder and fatal injuries. "The student," says the Vienna Statutes (1388), "shall not spend more time in drinking, fighting, and guitar playing than at physics, logic, and the regular course of lectures." "Swift once asked a young clergyman if he smoked. Being answered that he did not, 'It is a sign,' said he, 'you were not bred in the University of Oxford, for drinking and smoking are the first rudiments of learning taught there; and in these two arts no university in Europe can outdo them'" (The Atlantic Monthly, November, 1897).

55. P. 62. Quintilian, Inst. Orat., i, 3.
56. P. 63. Diogenes Laertius, iv, 1.
57. P. 63. Plato, Laws, viii. Women and girls are to take part in these contests also.
58. P. 64. Seneca, Epist., 90.
59. P. 65. Horace, Epist., i, xvii, 23; also, Diogenes Laert., ii.
60. P. 65. Horace, Epist., i, xvii., 25.
61. P. 66. Cicero, Tusc. Quæs., iv, 3.
62. P. 66. Plato was not born until more than one hundred years after Pythagoras. It was the latter who made this answer to Leo. Heraclides was a disciple of Plato.
63. P. 66. Diogenes Laertius, vi.
64. P. 67. Cicero, Tusc. Quæs, ii, 4.
65. P. 69. Horace, Ars Poetica, 311.
66. P. 69. Seneca, Controvers., iii.
67. P. 69. Cicero, De Finibus, iii, 5.
68. P. 70. Tacitus, Dialogue on Orators, 19.

69. P. 70. Plutarch, Apothegms of the Lacedæmonians.

70. P. 70. Plutarch, Instructions to Statesmen.

71. P. 71. Ridiculum Consulem. Cato did not ridicule Cicero's eloquence in general, but his abuse of it while consul. Cicero was one day pleading for Murena against Cato, and began to ridicule the gravest principles of the Stoic philosophy. Cato at this made the remark which Montaigne has quoted.

72. P. 71. Horace, Satire, i, 4, 8.

73. P. 71. Horace, Satire, i, 4, 58.

74. P. 72. Seneca, Epist., 40. For Ronsard and Du Bellay, see article on The French Mastery of Style, by Ferdinand Brunetière (The Atlantic Monthly, November, 1897). Also, Joachim du Bellay, in Pater's The Renaissance (New York, 1897).

75. P. 72. Seneca, Epist., 49.

76. P. 73. Diogenes Laertius, ii.

77. P. 73. Seneca, Epist., vii, 183.

78. P. 73. Cicero, Acad., iv, 24.

79. P. 73. Quintilian, viii, 3.

80. P. 73. Seneca, Epist., 59.

81. P. 74. Epitaph on Lucan in Fabricus, Biblioth Lat., ii, 16.

82. P. 74. Montaigne was misled by the common edition of Suetonius, which reads, " Eloquentia Militari; qua re aut æquavit." The later and better reading is, " Eloquentia, militarique re, aut æquavit,". which would seem to remove Montaigne's objection to it (Life of Cæsar, 55).

83. P. 75. Seneca, Epist., 40.

84. P. 75. Seneca, Epist., 75.

85. P. 75. Diogenes Laertius, x.

86. P. 78. See Stanislaus Arendt, Pensées de Mi-

chel de Montaigne en Matière d'education d'enfants (Sagan, 1889). These passages are also the basis of a little book by the Abbé Mangin, Education de Montaigne; ou L'Art d'enseigner le Latin à l'instar des mères latines (Paris, Didot, 1818). Locke put the idea into practice, and engaged a lady who could talk "Latin and Greek" to teach the child, Mr. Anthony, afterward the third Lord Shaftesbury.

87. P. 79. In regard to this passage von Raumer says (Geschichte, vol. i, p. 367 *et seq.*) : "Montaigne rightly exclaims against a joyless learning in which there is no love for anything. But he, and thousands in modern times who wish to avoid Charybdis fall into Scylla, in an enervating want of discipline and in an unmethodical method of teaching and learning. Their ideal is an Epicurean, enjoyable dilettantism from youth up, without that healthful severity of school life which forms strong, manly characters who learn from their studies how constantly to subordinate circumstances, to obey them, and to master them." This is a danger to be avoided, undoubtedly, and Montaigne seems reprehensible when the passage is taken alone. But compare pages 35–37, where Montaigne urges attention to the very ideas advocated by von Raumer. Plato approves of the Egyptian practice of teaching arithmetic in games (Laws, vii). Rabelais (Book i) made school life pleasant by using cards "not to play with, but to learn a thousand pretty tricks and new inventions which were all founded upon arithmetic."

88. P. 81. "A tale is the first key to the heart of a child," and our present movement, of placing fables and folk stories in the first grades of school, is in response to a deep need of the child mind. Locke suggests Æsop's Fables and Reynard the Fox (sec. 156).

Rousseau thinks Robinson Crusoe the best reading book to be put into the hands of a child. See also Dr. Felix Adler's admirable plan in The Moral Instruction of Children (New York, 1895).

89. P. 84. Virgil, Bucol., 8, 39.
90. P. 84. Livy, xxiv, 24.
91. P. 86. Locke thinks a pedant is made by learning "scraps of authors got by heart"; "than which there is nothing less becoming a gentleman" (sec. 175).
92. P. 87. Rabelais, Gargantua, i, 39, who quotes it from Plutarch, Life of Cicero.
93. P. 88. Montaigne is not quite exact in the sentiments which he ascribes to Plato, who simply says that the philosopher is so ignorant of what his neighbor does that he scarce knows whether he is a man or some other animal. Plato, Theætetus.
94. P. 89. Pacuvius, ap. Gellium, xiii, 8.
95. P. 90. Diogenes Laertius, vi.
96. P. 90. By βασιλεία is to be understood not royalty, but a particular office so styled at Ephesus, as well as at Athens and Rome, after they had discarded a monarchical form of government.
97. P. 91. Diogenes Laertius, ix.
98. P. 91. *Ibid.*, viii.
99. P. 91. Diogenes Laertius (in Vitâ) and Cicero in De Divinatione, i, 49, mention the speculation by which Thales made so much money. He bought up the olive trees in the Milesian fields before they were in bloom.
100. P. 92. Seneca, Epist., 88.
101. P. 93. Cicero, Tusc. Quæs., v, 36.
102. P. 94. Seneca, Epist., 108.
103. P. 94. Calvicius Sabinus, who lived in the time of Seneca. He bought slaves at a great price,

one who was master of Homer, another of Hesiod, and nine of lyric poetry. Seneca, Epist., 27.

104. P. 95. Plutarch, How a man should listen.

105. P. 95. Have we anywhere a more powerful and striking arraignment of mere word knowledge? Montaigne was the first to break away from the Renaissance ideal, learning, and place the stress upon the learner. Consult Joseph Kehr, "Die Erziehungs-Methode des Michael von Montaigne," Eupen, 1889.

106. P. 95. Cicero, Acad., ii, 1.

107. P. 95. Euripides, apud Cicero Epist. ad Fam., xiii, 15.

108. P. 96. Cicero, De Offic., iii, 15.

109. P. 96. Cicero, De Finib., i, 1.

110. P. 96. Juvenal, Sat., viii, 14.

111. P. 96. This reflection was made by Diogenes the Cynic according to Diogenes Laertius, vi. Coste's edition of Montaigne is the only one which does not say Dionysius.

112. P. 97. Plato, Protagoras.

113. P. 99. Persius, Sat., i, 61.

114. P. 100. Juvenal, Sat., xiv, 34.

115. P. 100. Apud Stobaeus, Litt., iii, 37.

116. P. 101. Seneca, Epist., 106.

117. P. 101. Cicero, Tusc. Quæs., ii, 4.

118. P. 101. The same thought is found in Molière, Les Femmes Savantes (act ii, scene 7). Here Montaigne again shows his limitations, which, however, are the limitations of his century. In Book iii, 3, he is even more severe upon women, especially upon those who would appear educated, and "speak and write after a new and learned way; and quote Plato and Aquinas, in things which the first man they meet could determine as well. The learning that can not penetrate

their minds hangs upon the tongue." ... "It is a great folly to put out their own light and shine by borrowed lustre." ... "It is because they do not sufficiently know themselves, or do themselves justice. The world has nothing fairer than they." ... "What need have they of anything but to live beloved and honored? But if, nevertheless, it angers them to give precedence to us in anything, and if they will insist upon having their share in books, poetry is a diversion proper for them. It is a lively, subtle, underhanded, and prating art — all show and pleasure like themselves. They may also get something from history. From the moral part of philosophy they may select such teachings as will help them to lengthen the pleasures of life and gently to bear the inconstancy of a lover, the rudeness of a husband, the burden of years, wrinkles, and the like. This is the utmost I would allow them in the sciences."

119. P. 102. Seneca, Epist., 95. Rousseau also expresses the same thought in Discours sur les Lettres.

120. P. 104. Cicero, De Nat. Deorum, v, 31. This whole passage is a strong plea for moral training. Gen. Brinkerhoff, president of the National Prison Congress, in his annual address for 1897, said, among other things: "First and foremost, what is most essential to be done is to revolutionize our educational system from top to bottom, so that good morals, good citizenship, and ability to earn an honest living shall be its primary purpose, instead of intellectual culture as heretofore."

121. P. 105. Cyropædia, i, 3.

122. P. 106. Plutarch, Apothegms; also Rousseau, Discours sur les Lettres.

123. P. 107.   Plutarch, Lives, Agesilaus.

124. P. 108.   Plato, Hippias Major. This work attributed to Plato is considered by Jowett spurious and is not included in his edition of 1892.

125. P. 109.   Philip Camerarius, Medit. Hist. Cent., iii, 31. Also Rousseau in Discours sur les Lettres.

126. P. 110.   The essay, of which this forms a part, was addressed to Madame D'Estissac, whose son accompanied Montaigne on his journey to Rome.

127. P. 112.   Aristotle, Ethics, ix, 7.

128. P. 113.   Montaigne had no personal love for the child he would educate. He took no great pride in his own children, nor would he have mourned had he been childless. "The births of our intelligence are the children most truly our own, ... and who would not be much prouder to be father to the Æneid than to the handsomest youth of Rome?" (Essays, ii, 8).

129. P. 115.   Aristotle, Ethics, iv, 3.

130. P. 115.   Terence, Adelph., i, 40.

131. P. 116.   The only instance in the Essays where Montaigne uses "Education" instead of "Institution" or "Nourriture."

132. P. 116.   The Essayist again speaks of his daughter in Book iii, chapter v. She was afterward married to Viscount de Gamaches.

133. P. 117.   Livy, xxviii, 28.

134. P. 118.   Madame de Sévigné in her Letters says she never read this passage without tears in her eyes. "Dear me," she exclaims, "how full of good sense is this book!"

135. P. 119.   Montaigne here refers to the death of his dearest friend, la Boëtie. See further, Book i, chapter xxvii, Of Friendship, his finest essay.

136. P. 120. Cæsar, De Bello Gall., vi, 18.

137. P. 122. Montaigne has here in mind the use Plato makes of the words we translate finite and infinite. See Jowett's Introduction to the Philebus Dialogues of Plato (New York, 1892), where he explains that the finite comprises what admits of measure (i. e. definite), the infinite what admits of degrees (i. e. indefinite). Spinoza, also, in his Ethica ordine mathematico demonstrata, speaks of Good as something real and positive; Evil nothing real, but only the negation of Good.

138. P. 123. Plutarch, Life of Lysander.

139. P. 124. Diogenes Laertius, in Life of Plato, gives this anecdote, but he does not say that it was a a boy playing at nuts, but a man playing at dice, which would make Plato's rejoinder far more effective.

140. P. 124. Locke, in sections 34, 35, 36, gives a paraphrase of what Montaigne here says about training in cruelty and vanity. See also Der Einfluss Montaigne's auf die Pädagogischen Ansichten von Joh. Locke (C. M. Mehner, Leip., 1891).

141. P. 126. Here we have, it seems to me, the sixteenth-century germ of the kindergarten. Rabelais recognized the value of games in teaching, as did also Locke and Rousseau. It is only within our own decade, however, that the amusements of children have been subjected to scientific attention or considered worthy of it. See the careful work of Mr. George E. Johnson, A Study of the Educational Value of One Thousand Classified Plays and Games (published by Swan, Sonnenschein & Co.). Since 1893 Dr. Stoyan Tsanoff has shown tireless activity in working out his great object—character-building through play. It is

through play, inseparable from school instruction, that Dr. Tsanoff would lead the child out into a larger and stronger life. "Next to hereditary disposition and gifts," he says, "it is through play that the child develops that life, energy, and quickening of spirit which scatter dullness, stupidity, and melancholy in the subsequent man. Play is but the breathing of the soul, it not only strengthens, it also sweetens life." And, quoting Froebel, Education of Man, he adds: "A child that plays thoroughly, with self-active determination, persevering until physical fatigue forbids, will surely be a thoroughly determined man, capable of self-sacrifice for the promotion of the welfare of himself and others." A. C. Haddon, in The Study of Man (New York, 1898), throws much light upon the origin of children's plays, and indicates that it is the child who is the true conservative. The Play of Animals, by Karl Groos (New York, 1899), seeks to establish the conception of play on a basis of natural science. The play of animals is necessary to fit them for the tasks of later life. "Animals do not play because they are young, but they have their youth because they must play." Dr. Groos suggests many resemblances between animal plays and those of children. Der Spiele des Menschen, by the same author, will be eagerly awaited by all interested in this important subject.

142. P. 128. Diogenes Laertius. Also Horace, Satire, ii, 3, 235.

143. P. 129. Lactant. Divin. Instit., iii, 5.

144. P. 130. "Conceive the modern educational methods to have been applied to that stock of moral truths which all good men accept, and you will have the material for the moral lessons which are needed in

a public school" (Dr. Felix Adler, The Moral Instruction of Children).

145. P. 131. Seneca, Epist., 106.
146. P. 132. Tacitus, Life of Agricola, iv.
147. P. 133. Seneca, Epist., 106.
148. P. 134. Aristotle, Ethics, x, 9.
149. P. 135. Juvenal, Satire, vi, 648.
150. P. 135. Juvenal, Satire, xiv, 70.
151. P. 137. Ovid, De Arte, iii, 503.
152. P. 137. Suetonius, Life of Cæsar, 12.
153. P. 138. Cicero, De Finibus, i, 19.
154. P. 139. Seneca, Epist., 33.
155. P. 140. This, in connection with pages 26 and 27, 101 and 102, seems to indicate that Montaigne would be out of sympathy with an educational system having a democratic basis. In a way, however, he contradicts these statements on page 128. Some excuse this pro-monarchic tendency because of the time in which Montaigne lived, and I wish to call the attention of these to an article by Prof. H. T. Peck in The Cosmopolitan (July, 1897). "Not every one is capable of being educated." "What the State needs above all," says Professor Peck, "is an aristocracy of well-trained university men to drive in harness the hewers of wood and drawers of water who constitute the vast majority of the human race. . . . For every really great thing that has been accomplished in the history of man has been accomplished by an aristocracy." In this line also is the remark attributed to Prof. C. E. Norton, of Harvard University, apropos of the Spanish-American war, that the mission of the educated is to minister to the lower classes of society, and let the uneducated do the fighting.

156. P. 141. Horace, Ars Poetica, 7.

157. P. 142. Martial, vii, 73.
158. P. 145. Seneca, Epist., 123.
159. P. 150. " Les faits changent de forme dans la tête de l'historien ; ils se moulent sur ses intérêts, ils prennent la teinte de ses prejugés " (Rousseau, Émile, iv).

INDEX OF NAMES.

Academica (Cicero), notes 23, 78, 106.
Academy of Ferrara, note 37.
Adelphi (Terence), note 130.
Adler, Felix, notes 88, 144.
Æneid (Virgil), 82; notes 32, 128.
Æsop's Fables, note 88.
Agesilaus, 106, 107; note 123.
Agricola, note 146.
Agrigentines, 91.
Agrippa, note 15.
Alaric, note 15.
Albrecht of Saxony, note 54.
Alcibiades, 65.
Alexander, 58, 63, 64.
Alexandrides, 44.
Amadis de Gaul, 81.
American, xv, 13.
Anacreon, note 85.
Anaxagoras, 91.
Anaximenes, 50.
Angelica, 54.
Anthony, Mr., note 86.
Antipater, 107.
Aper, 70.
Apollo, 63.
Apollodorus, 22.
Apothegms (Plutarch), notes 28, 69, 122.
Aquinas, note 118.
Arabic, 78.
Arcesilaus, 28.
Archimedes, 90.

Arendt, Stanislaus, note 86.
Ariosto, note 42.
Aristippus, 38, 65, 73, 104.
Aristo, 84, 103.
Aristophanes, 75.
Aristotelian, 80, 112.
Aristotle, 13, 20, 30, 31, 57, 91, 94, 115, 134, 144.
  (Commentary on, by Guerento), 78.
  (Ethics), notes 127, 129, 148.
  (Treatise on Temperance), 57.
Arndt, Theodor, note 14.
Arnold, Matthew, 9; note 8.
Arnold, Thomas, note 8.
Arnstädt, Dr. F. A., 14; note 54.
Ars Poetica (Horace), notes 65, 156.
Asia, 43.
A Study of the Educational Value of One Thousand Classified Plays and Games (Johnson), note 141.
Astyages, 105.
Atlantic Monthly, notes 54, 74.
Athenians, 70, 76, 107.
Athens, 44, 70, 106; note 96.

Baralipton (figure of logic), 53.
Baroco (figure of logic), 53.
Basedow, 16.
βασιλεία, note 96.
Beauregard, 5.
Bibliothek Lat., note 81.

171

Black Prince, 1.
Boccaccio, 57.
Boëtie, Etienne de la, 3, 4, 43; notes 27, 135.
  (Voluntary Servitude), 3, 43; note 27.
Boniface IV, Pope, note 15.
Bonn, note 40.
Book of the Dead, 13.
Bordeaux, 3, 4, 68; note 4.
  Huon of, 81.
  University of, 6.
Bradamante, 54.
Brinckerhoff, General, note 120.
Brissac, Count de, 79.
  Marshal de, 79.
Brittany, Duke of, 101.
Brunetière, F., note 74.
Buchanan, George, 78, 79, 84.
Bucolics (Virgil), note 89.

Cæsar, 41, 74, 120, 137, 144, 148.
  De Bello Gallico, note 136.
  Life of, by Suetonius, notes 82, 152.
Calisthenes, 64.
Calvinists, 5.
Camerarius, Philip, note 125.
Candale, Francis, Lord of, 27.
Capricornus, 49.
Carneades, 59.
Caracci, Annibale, note 15.
Carthage, 42.
Catholics, 5.
Cato, 71; note 71.
Charlemagne, 41.
Charles VIII, 109.
  IX, 4.
Charybdis, note 87.
Chassagne, Françoise de la, 4.
Chesterfield, Lord, note 54.
Chinese, 13.
Chios, Aristo of, 103.
Christian, 5, 101; notes 8, 15.

Christianity, 5.
Chronique Gargantuine (Rabelais), 2; note 92.
Chrysippus, 22, 73; note 2.
Cicero, 33, 57, 71, 94, 95, 144, 148; notes 71, 92.
  Academica, notes 23, 78, 106.
  De Divinatione, note 99.
  De Finibus, notes 67, 109, 153.
  De Natura Deorum, notes 9, 120.
  De Officiis, notes 22, 108.
  Epistles, note 107.
  Tusculariarum Quæstionum or Disputationum, notes 16, 18, 20, 61, 64, 101, 117.
Cleanthes, 20, 73.
Cleomenes, 70.
Cléry, 68.
College of Guyenne, 80.
College of Montagu, note 54.
  of Navarre, note 54.
Comenius, 13-17.
Comic Homer, 2.
Commentary on Aristotle (Guerente), 78.
Compayré (Histoire de la Pédagogie), xv.
Conseiller, 3.
Controvers. (Seneca), note 66.
Cosmopolitan Magazine, note 155.
Coste, 13; note 111.
Cotton, xvi, 24.
Courbet, xvi.
Crates, 90.
Crete, 76.
Cretans, 134.
Cyclops, 134.
Cymon, 25.
Cyropædia, note 121.
Cyrus, 105.

Danaides, 20.
Dante (Inferno), note 12.
Declaration of Independence, 10.

INDEX OF NAMES. 173

De Arte (Ovid), note 151.
De Bello Gallico (Cæsar), note 136.
De Comitiis Romanorum (Grouchy), 78.
De Divinatione (Cicero), note 99.
De Finibus (Cicero), notes 67, 109, 153.
De Natura Deorum (Cicero), notes 9, 120.
De Officiis (Cicero), notes 22, 108.
Delphi, Temple of, 51.
Demetrius, 51.
Demophoön, 63.
Der Einfluss Montaigne's auf die Pädagogischen Ansichten von Joh. Locke (Mehner), note 140.
Der Spiele des Menschen (Groos), note 141.
D'Estissac, Madame, 110; note 126.
Monsieur, 111.
Dialogue on Orators (Tacitus), note 68.
Didot, note 86.
Die Erziehungsmethode des Michel von Montaigne (Kehr), note 105.
Diogenes Laertius, 147; notes 2, 3, 36, 48, 49, 56, 59, 63, 76, 85, 95, 97-99, 111, 139, 142.
(Chrysippus), note 2.
(Epicurus), note 3.
(Life of Plato), note 139.
Diogenes the Cynic, 66; note 111.
Dionysius, 96; note 111.
Discourse on the Power of the Imagination (Plutarch), 21.
Discours sur les Lettres (Rousseau), notes 119, 122, 125.
Divinæ Institutiones (Lactantius), note 143.
Dresden, note 14.
Du Bellay, 72, 86; note 74.

Education de Montaigne (Abbé Mangin), note 86.
Education (Spencer), note 5.
Educational Reformers (Quick), xi.
Egyptian, note 87.
Émile (Rousseau), 15; notes 8, 159.
Empedocles, 91.
England, 8.
English, xv, 14.
Ennius, 96.
Ephesus, note 96.
Ephesians, 91.
Epicharmus, 32.
Epicurus, 22, 58, 75; note 3.
Epicureans, 31.
Epistles (Cicero), note 107.
(Horace), notes 33, 52, 59, 60.
(Seneca), notes 11, 13, 21, 53, 74, 75, 77, 80, 83, 84, 100, 102, 103, 116, 119, 145, 147, 154, 158.
Erasmus, xv; note 54.
Ethics (Aristotle), notes 127, 129, 148.
(Spinoza), note 137.
Euganean, 96.
Eupen, note 105.
Euripides, note 107.
Medea, 22.
Europe, notes 37, 54.
Eyquem, 1, 2.
Michel, 1.
Pierre, 2.

Fabricius, note 81.
Fénelon, 15-17.
Ferrara, Academy of, note 37.
Fitch, Dr., note 8.
Flora, 16, 63.
Florence, 2.
Florio, xvi.
Foix, Counts of, 27.
Mme. Diane de, 19.
France, 1, 5, 7, 8, 45, 59, 65, 70, 77, 78, 81, 84, 102, 112; note 54.

Francis, Duke of Brittany, 101.
　Lord of Candale, 27.
　II, 4.
François Rabelais und sein Traité d'Éducation (Arnstädt), 14; note 54.
French, xvi, 2, 14, 19, 22, 34, 59, 72, 74, 78, 122, 148, 150; notes 8, 16.
Froebel, 15–17; notes 16, 45.
　Education of Man, note 141.
Froissart, 149.

Galen, 98.
Gamaches, Viscount de, note 132.
Gascon, 74, 94.
Gaul, Amadis de, 81.
Gauls, 120.
Gaza, Theodore, 59; note 37.
Gellium (Pacuvium), note 94.
Genseric, note 15.
Germanicus, 63.
Germany, 4, 7, 8, 65.
German, xv, 14, 77.
Geschichte (von Raumer), note 37.
Gorgons, 137.
Goths, 108.
Gourney, Mlle. de, note 43.
Goveanus, Andreas, 84.
Graces, 16, 63.
Greece, 5, 84, 106, 108.
Grecian, 86.
Greek, 11, 14, 76, 79, 92, 97, 100, 128, 151; notes 37, 54.
Greeks, 77, 89, 108.
Groos, Karl, note 141.
Grouchy, Nicholas, 78.
Grun, xvi.
Guerente, William, 78, 84.
Gurson, Mme. Diane de Foix, Countess of, 19.
Guyenne, 1.
　College of, 80, 84.

Haddon, A. C., note 141.

Hannibal, 42.
Harvard, University of, note 155.
Hegesias, 66.
Henry III, 4.
Henry IV, 2.
Heraclides Ponticus, 66; note 62.
Heracleon, the Megarean, 52.
Heraclitus, 90.
Herbart, note 10.
Herbartian, 11; notes 10, 14, 45.
Hercules, 69.
Hesiod, notes 41, 103.
Hesperian, 49.
Hindoos, 13.
Hippias, 107, 108.
　Major (Plato), note 124.
Hippocrates, 135.
Hispanus, Peter, note 40.
Histoire de la Pédagogie (Compayré), xv.
History of Logical Teaching, Ueberweg, note 40.
Hobbes, note 50.
Homer, 94; note 103.
　Comic, 2.
Horace, 71.
　Ars Poetica, notes 65, 156.
　Epistles, notes 33, 52, 59, 60.
　Odes, note 17.
　Satires, notes 72, 73, 142.
Huon of Bordeaux, 81.
How a Man should Listen (Plutarch), note 104.

Inferno (Dante), note 12.
Institutiones Oratoriæ (Quintilian), note 55.
Instructions to Statesmen (Plutarch), note 70.
Ionia, 65.
Isabella of Scotland, 101.
Isocrates, 59.
Italy, 2, 4, 34, 78, 80, 109; note 15.
Italian, 42, 82, 86.

INDEX OF NAMES. 175

Jena, University of, note 54.
John V, 101.
Johnson, George E., note 141.
Journey into Italy (Montaigne), note 15.
Jowett (Plato, edition of), notes 6, 124, 137.
Juvenal (Satires), notes 39, 110, 114, 149, 150.

Kehr, Joseph, note 105.

Lacedæmon, 106.
Lacedæmonians, 42, 65, 67, 76, 134.
Lactantius (Divinæ Institutiones), note 143.
Laertius, Diogenes, 147; notes, 2, 3, 36, 48, 49, 56, 59, 63, 76, 85, 95, 97, 98, 99, 111, 139, 142.
Lamennais, 3.
Lancelot du Lac, 81.
Latin, 11, 14, 76, 77, 78, 79, 81, 84, 92, 97, 128, 139, 150; notes 1, 54, 86.
Latinist, 67.
Laws (Plato), notes 57, 87.
Lehrplan, 8.
Leipzig, 14, 54; note 140.
Leo, 49, 66; note 62.
Le Paluel, 33.
Leonora, 116.
Les Femmes Savantes (Molière), note 118.
Livia, Signora, 34.
Lives (Plutarch), 42; notes 92, 123, 138.
Livy, 43; notes 90, 133.
Locke, John, xv, 1, 13, 14, 15, 16, 17; notes 8, 16, 19, 20, 46, 54, 86, 88, 91, 140, 141.
 Some Thoughts concerning Education, 13, 15.
London, xvi, 15.
Lucan, note 81.
Lucullus, 95.

Luther, notes 16, 45.
Lycurgus, 104, 134.
Lysander (Plutarch), note 138.

MacAlister, Dr., xvi.
Madeira, Island of, 118.
Maestro del Sacro Palasso, 4.
Mangin, Abbé (Education de Montaigne), note 86.
Marcellus, 42.
Marguerite de Navarre, 2.
Marshal de Brissac, 79.
Marshal de Montluc, 118, 119.
Martial, note 157.
Massiliensis, Salvianus, 122.
Mayors, 3, 4.
Medea (Euripides), 22.
Medici, Catherine de, 4.
Megarean, Heracleon the, 52.
Mehner, C. M., note 140.
Monœceus, 58.
Menander, 72.
Menge, note 15.
Metamorphoses (Ovid), 8.
Milesian, note 99.
Milton, 3.
Minerva, 63.
Molière (Les Femmes Savantes), note 118.
Montaigne, xv, 1, 2, 3, 4, 5, 7, 8, 9, 10, 11, 12, 13, 14, 15, 16, 17, 18; notes 1, 4, 6, 8, 14, 15, 16, 19, 20, 25, 37, 40, 43, 46, 54, 71, 82, 86, 87, 93, 105, 111, 118, 126, 128, 131, 135, 137, 140, 155.
Montaigne's Ideen über Erziehung (Arndt), note 15.
Montaigne (Journey into Italy), note 15.
Montaigne, Life of (Bayle St. John), xvi.
 (Of Friendship), note 135.
 (Reimer's), xv.

Montagu, College of, note 54.
Montluc, Marshal de, 118, 119.
Moors, note 54.
Mulcaster, 13.
Murel, Mark Antony, 78.
Murena, note 71.
Muret, 84.
Muses, 27, 63, 104.

Naigeon, M., note 43.
Naples, 109.
National Prison Congress, note 120.
Navarre, Marguerite de, 2.
  College of, note 54.
Nero, 34.
New York, 15; notes 8, 74, 88, 137, 141.
Norton, Prof. C. E., note 155.
Numa, 134.

Ode (Anacreon), note 85.
  Horace, note 17.
Of Friendship (Montaigne), note 135.
Olympic Games, 47.
On Exile (Plutarch), note 29.
On False Shame (Plutarch), note 26.
On Oracles which have ceased (Plutarch), note 38.
Orlando Furioso (Ariosto), note 42.
Orleans, 68.
Ovid, 81.
  De Arte, note 151.
  Metamorphoses, 81.
Oxford, University of, note 54.

Pacuvius (Gellium), note 94.
Pädagogische Bibliothek, xv.
Pantagruel (Rabelais), 2.
Pantheon, note 15.
Paris, xvi, 2, 4, 75, notes 27, 86.
Parthians, 103.
Pasquier, 6.
Pater (The Renaissance), note 74.
Pau, 2.

Payen, xvi.
Payne, 15.
Peck, Prof. H. T., note 155.
Pensées de Michel Montaigne, etc. (Arendt), note 86.
Périgord, 1.
Perigordian, 78, 97.
Persia, 50.
Persians, 13, 65, 104.
Persius, notes 31, 45, 47, 113.
Pestalozzi, 15, 16, 17; note 16.
Petit-Pont, 69.
Philebus (Plato), note 137.
Philiasians, 66.
Phocas, Emperor, note 15.
Phrygia, 54.
Physical Education (Spencer), note 19.
Pindar, 122.
Pisa, 30.
Plato, 13, 25, 30, 31, 32, 33, 42, 56, 60, 61, 63, 66, 76, 94, 97, 103, 104, 105, 122, 124; notes 6, 62, 87, 93, 118, 137, 139.
  (Hippias Major), note 124.
  (Jowett's edition of), notes 6, 124, 137.
  (Laws), notes 57, 87.
  (Life of, by Diogenes Laertius), note 139.
  (Philebus), note 137.
  (Protagoras), note 112.
  (Republic), 25, 103, 122; notes 7, 44.
  (Theages), note 6.
  (Theætetus), note 93.
Platonic, 89.
Plautus, 82.
Plutarch, 20, 43, 44, 57, 86, 134, 147; notes 26, 28, 29.
  (Agesilaus), note 123.
  (Apothegms), notes 28, 69, 122.
  (Discourse on the Powers of the Imagination), 21.

INDEX OF NAMES. 177

Plutarch, (How a Man should Listen), note 104.
  (Instructions to Statesmen), note 70.
  (Lives), 42; notes 92, 123, 138.
  (Lysander), note 138.
  (On Exile), note 29.
  (On False Shame), note 26.
  (On Oracles that have Ceased), note 38.
  (Symposium), note 51.
Polemon, 128.
Polycrates, 70.
Pompey, 33.
Ponticus, Heraclides, 66; note 62.
Propertius, notes 24, 34.
Protagoras (Plato), 97; note 112.
Protestants, 5.
Pythagoras, 47, 50; note 62.
Pythagoreans, 122.

Quick, Edition of Locke, "Thoughts," etc., 13, 15.
Educational Reformers, xv.
Quintilian, 13, 62; note 79.
  Institutiones Oratoriæ, note 55.

Rabelais, François, xv, 18; notes 54, 87, 141.
  Arnstadt's. 14; note 54.
  Chronique Gargantuine, 2; note 92.
  Comic Homer, 2.
  Pantagruel, 2.
Rabirius, Caius, 137.
Raphael, note 15.
Ratich, 14, 16.
Raumer, von, note 87.
Reimer (Michael v. Montaigne), xv.
Renaissance, 14; note 104.
Republic (Plato), 95, 103; notes 7, 44.
Reynard the Fox, note 82.
Richter, 16.
Rittershusius Joannes Phil.

Rochefoucauld, Comte de la, 68.
Rome, 2, 4, 31, 108; notes 15, 96, 126, 128.
Roman, 94, 151.
Romans, 77, 86.
Ronsard, 72; note 74.
Rousseau, xv, 3, 10, 13, 14, 15, 16, 17; notes 1, 8, 16, 19, 25, 88, 141.
  Confessions, note 1.
  Discours sur les Lettres, notes 119, 122, 125.
  Émile, 15; notes, 8, 159.
Royer, xvi.

Sabinus, Calvicius, note 103.
Sagan, note 86.
Sallust, 148.
Samos, 70.
Santa Rotunda, 34; note 15.
Satire (Horace), notes 72, 73, 142.
  Juvenal, notes, 89, 110, 114, 149, 150.
  Persius, note 113.
Savoy, Duke of, 45.
Savoyard, 45.
Saxony, Albrecht, Duke of, note 54.
Scipio, 42.
Schoolmen, 53.
Scotland, Isabella of, 101.
Scottish, 78.
Scylla, note 87.
Scythians, 108.
Sebonde, Ramondus de (Theologia Naturalis), 4.
Seneca, 20, 94, 95; note 103.
  Controvers., note 66.
  Epistles, notes 11, 13, 21, 58, 74, 76, 77, 80, 83, 84, 100, 102, 103, 113, 116, 144, 147, 148, 158.
  Reisigius, Mnio., do, note 134.
  Shaftsbury, note 23.
Silly, 107.
Simplicius, 22, 83, 43, 48, 53, 88, 107, 130, 134, 150.

*Solar Family, note 1.
Some Thoughts concerning Education (Locke), 13, 15.
Sophists, 57, 97.
Spanish-American War, note 155.
Sparta, 65, 70, 107.
Spartans, 107.
Spencer (Education), note 5.
 (Physical Education), note 19.
Speusippus, 63.
Spinoza (Ethics), note 137.
St. Bartholomew, 5.
St. Innocent, note 54.
St. John, Bayle (Life of Montaigne), xvi.
Stobæus, note 115.
Stoic, note 71.
Stoics, 31.
Suetonius, 74, 137; note 82.
 Life of Cæsar, notes 82, 152.
Swift, note 54.
Switzerland, 4.
Symposium (Plutarch), note 51.
Syracuse, 90.
System of Logic (Ueberweg), note 40.

Tacitus, 70, 131.
Tacitus (Agricola), note 146.
 (Dialogue on Orators), note 68.
Talmud, 13.
Tamerlane, 108.
Tartars, note 54.
Tasso (Torquato), 26.
Terence, 82.
Terence (Adelphi), note 130.
Thales, 91; note 99.
Theages (Plato), note 6.
Theætetus (Plato), note 93.
The French Mastery of Style (Brunetière), note 74.
Themistocles, 25.
The Moral Instruction of Children (Adler), notes 88, 144.

Theologia Naturalis (Ramondus Sebonde), 4.
The Play of Animals (Groos), note 141.
The Renaissance (Pater), note 74.
The Study of Man (Haddon), note 141.
Titan, 100.
Treatise on Intemperance (Aristotle), 57.
Tsanoff, Dr. Stoyan, note 141.
Turks, 108.
Turnebus, Adrian, 99.
Tuscany, 109.
Tusculanarum Quæstionum (Cicero), notes 16, 18, 30, 61, 64, 101, 117.

Ueberweg (History of Logical Teaching), note 40.
 (System of Logic), note 40.
Ulysses, 96.
United States, 9, 10.
University of Bordeaux, 6.
 Harvard, note 155.
 Jena, note 54.
 Oxford, note 54.
 Yale, note 53.

Valentinianus (Emperor), 122.
Vienna, Statutes of, note 54.
Virgil (Æneid), 82; notes 32, 128.
 (Bucolics), note 89.
Voluntary Servitude (La Boëtie), 3, 43; note, 27.

Westminster School, note 54.
Westphalian, 72.

Xenocrates, 128.
Xenophon, 31, 104, 105, 107.

Yale (University), note 53.

Zeno, 76, 104.
Zeuxidamus, 67.

GENERAL INDEX.

Ability, education should be according to, 56, 102, 103.
for action lacking in pedants, but great in real philosophers, 89-92.
versus mere learning and material circumstances, 87-89.
Action, ability for, great in philosophers, 90.
ability for, lacking in pedants, 89.
more important than mere philosophy and memorizing, 66, 67, 86-89.
Actions speak louder than words, 66, 67, 106, 107.
Adaptability commended, 64, 65.
of Alcibiades, 65.
the aim of education, 8.
"Æque pauperibus," etc. (Horace), 60.
Affectation, avoid, 73-75.
Affection, arouse, for virtue, 54.
of children should be held by virtue and wisdom, 115.
parental, 19.
parental, greater than filial, 112.
real, not shown by excessive caresses, 113, 114.
Age, venerable, 115.
" A great boy," etc. (Cyrus), 105.
" Alter ab undecimo," etc. (Virgil), 84.

Amusements, government should provide certain, 85.
share children's, 117.
Anger leads to cruelty, 135.
leads to injustice, 136, 137.
Apperception, Herbartian, foreshadowed, 11, 18, 29; notes 10, 14.
not mere memorizing, 33.
Appetite, restrain, within limits, 64.
should not be pampered, 144, 145.
"Apud alios loqui," etc. (Cicero), 93.
Aristocracy of learning, note 155.
" Aristoni tragico actori," etc. (Livy), 84.
Arithmetic taught by games, 79.
Art, answer of Heraclides against, 66.
to learn the arts is not all of philosophy, 66.
" δεύτεvs, ex," etc. (Cyropædia), 104.
" As to your exordium," etc. (Cleomenes), 70.
Authority of nature imperative, 112.
maintained by austerity condemned, 118, 119.
maintained by wealth condemned, 115.
" Aut qui non verba," etc. (Quintilian), 73.

THE EDUCATION OF CHILDREN.

Aversions, train against, 63, 64, 144, 145.
"Because we would," etc. (Zeuxidamus), 67.
Better-learned preferable to more learned, 92.
Book learning alone of no value, 14, 19, 58, 59, 66, 85, 93–94, 139.
"Bouha prou bouha," etc. (Gascon proverb), 94.
Brevity not always a virtue, 43, 44.
study, 39.
Buying brains, 94.

Character, development of, 7.
first aim of education, 17, 48–50, 54, 66, 92, 123.
Cheating a childish habit, 125.
guard against, in games, 125, 126.
Cheerfulness a sign of wisdom, 52, 53.
"Che non men," etc. (Dante), note 12.
Children's rights, 113, 114.
Child study, 11, 29.
Class distinctions, Montaigne and Locke conscious of, 1.
Plato's idea of, note 7.
Clothes not the man, 99, 100.
College condemned, 59, 60, 61–62, 78, 81.
evils of, note 54.
Hobbes' opinion of, note 50.
Latinist has no practical knowledge, 67, 68.
Concentration commended, 141, 142.
Conscience necessary for justice, 101.
should be shown in speech, 40.
should be trained, 92.
Constitution of the mind a factor in education, 25, 28, 29, 56, 81, 82, 102, 103, 124, 125; note 7.

Contention is base, 40.
"Contorta et aculeata," etc. (Cicero), 73.
Co-ordination, 11, 29; note 10.
Courtiers untrustworthy, 40.
Cowardliness increased by physical punishment, 116.
Cruelty, a childish habit, 124, 125.
caused by anger, 136.
Locke against, note 140.
of pedants, 61.
practised in colleges, 62.
Curiosity, cultivate honest, 41, 42.
Custom, should be transgressed by the great only, 33.

Debt of Locke and Rousseau to Montaigne, 14.
Decoration of school-rooms, 11, 62, 63.
Democracy, perhaps unfavourable to education, 9, 10, 12.
"Deprendas animi," etc. (Juvenal), 52.
Development of character, 7.
of the individual, 8, 11, 12, 29, 48, 102, 103; note 44.
should be general, 67, 127, 128.
Dice, anecdote of, note 139.
Difficulty of descending to child's level, 29.
Discipline of a tutor checked by home influences, 37.
should be applied with discretion, 121.
should be without physical violence, 61, 62, 116, 135–137.
violent, distasteful to Montaigne, 78, 83, 116.
Disposition a factor in education, 28, 29, 56, 103; note 7.
Montaigne's, 80, 82, 83.
of children variable, 25.
Disputation, avoid, 38.

Disputation, be fair in, 39.
Dissimulation a quality of Montaigne's time, 122, 123.
Dogmatism, unfruitful, 9, 10.
Domestic affairs should be imparted to children when of a suitable age, 114.

"Early but does," etc. (French proverb), 59.
Education, a continuous experiment, 9.
 aim of, 7.
 books on, printed mainly in German, xv.
 contrast between Athenian and Spartan systems of, 106, 108.
 everyone susceptible to, 6, 128.
 formal, condemned, 107.
 history of, parallel to that of religion, 9.
 in France, Germany, England, and the United States, 8.
 meaning of, 8.
 Montaigne's own, 1, 2, 77-79.
 Montaigne's single use of the word, 116; note 131.
 Montaigne the founder of a school of thinkers on, xv.
 of children, the most important and difficult of human effort, 25, 107.
 Persian system of, 104-106.
 problem of, solvable through the human, 12.
 reformatory, 128.
 should be by the State, 134, 145.
 should be enjoyable, 79.
 should be practical, 17, 13, 49, 50, 57, 58, 91, 92, 98, 99, 100.
 should make us better, 100.
 should not aim at gain, 27, 101, 102.

Education, Socrates' advice concerning, note 6.
"Either I am," etc. (Demetrius), 51, 52.
Eloquence, Cato's ridicule of Cicero's, 71; note 71.
 should not call attention to itself, 75.
"Emunctæ naris," etc. (Horace), 71.
Enjoyment of study and duty, 79.
 train for, 7.
Environment, human, physical, and social, 7.
Errors should be acknowledged, 39, 40.
"Et errat longe," etc. (Terence), 115.
"Et quo quemque," etc. (Virgil), 48.
Experience the best teacher if reflected on, 144.
Expression easy if ideas are clear, 68.

Familiarity, Marshal de Montluc's lack of, 118, 119.
 of parents with children advised, 117-118, 119-120.
Family, authority in the, maintained by austerity, 118, 119.
 authority in the, maintained by wealth, 115.
 importance of, in education shown by Froebel and Pestalozzi, note 16.
 life of Montaigne, Locke, and Rousseau limited, note 16.
 relations of Montaigne pleasant, 119.
Fault-finding, opposed, 38, 121.
Fear, contempt of, taught Alexander by Aristotle, 57.
 philosophy an enemy of, 48.
 philosophy teaches to what extent one should, evils, 53.

Fear of shame not induced by frequent punishment, 61, 62.
study should not induce, 58, 62.
Finite, Plato's meaning of, note 137.

Geometry not much taught by Aristotle, 57.
taught by games, 79.
Giving more enjoyable than receiving, 112, 113.
Grammar despised by Spartans, 106, 107.
knowledge of, not necessary for pure speech, 96.
grammarian no gentleman, 68.
grammarians ridiculed by Dionysius, 96.
"Gratum est," etc. (Juvenal), 135.
Greek insufficient to educate alone, 96, 97.
should be taught after the vernacular, 7, 14, 76.
taught as a game, 79.
too much time spent in acquiring, 76.

Habit, uncorrected in childhood leads to great evil, 124, 125.
Plato's opinion of, 124 : note 139.
"Habit is not," etc. (Plato), 124.
"Hæc demum sapiet," etc. (Epitaph on Lucan), 74.
"Hanc amplissimam," etc. (Cicero), 66.
History, a means of placing the child in relation to his environment, 7.
a mere language study to some, to others an anatomy of philosophy, 43.
classes of historians, 148–150.
clergymen and philosophers should not write, 152.

History deals more safely with the past than the present, 152.
eye-witnesses make the best historians, 150, 151.
importance of, 17.
middle class of historians leave little to the individual judgment, 149, 150.
Montaigne advocates Herbartian aim of, 11.
Montaigne's chief study, 20.
Montaigne's estimate of Cæsar, 147, 148.
Montaigne's estimate of Froissart, 150.
Montaigne's estimate of Laertius, 147.
Plutarch, Montaigne's favourite historian, 147.
Plutarch's valuable contribution to, 43.
point of view influenced by the occupation of the historian, 151, 152.
point of view influenced by the personality of the historian, note 159.
properly used a most valuable study, 42.
reasons for Montaigne's delight in, 148, 149.
rumours the transformed material of, 149.
should portray character, 42.
should train judgment, 43.
taught by biography, 147; note 25.
the only study of the Lacedæmonians, 42.
Honestum, 113.
Humanity, complexity of, 10.

Idleness condemned, 141.
"I know neither art," etc. (Heraclides), 66.

Imitation of words easy, of thoughts difficult, 75, 76.
Inclinations, evil, should be checked early, 124, 125.
   in reading should be fostered, 81, 82.
   natural, should be considered, 25, 28, 29, 56, 103; note 7.
   of children variable, 25.
   shou'd be controlled by reason, 113.
Indifference, personal, of Montaigne to children, note 128.
Individuality, 7, 11, 12, 29, 48.
Inflexibility, 9.
Influence of Italy, Pau, and Rabelais on the education of Henry of Navarre, Montaigne and others, 2.
   of La Boëtie, 3, 4.
   of Sebonde's "Theologia Naturalis," 4, 5.
   of the occupation of authors on histories, 151, 152.
   of wrong habits in childhood, 121, 124, 125.
   pupils are like masters, 93.
Information should be more sought than volunteered, 37.
Instruction can be gained from everyone, 41.
   everyone susceptible to, 6, 128.
   private, advocated, 14.
Intemperance, general, a characteristic of the human race, 131.
   in letters, 131, 132.
Intercourse, with men commended, 34, 44.
   should be general, 41.
"Ipsæ res verba," etc. (Cicero), 69.
"Is it not better," etc. (Heraclitus), 91.
"I therefore pretend," etc. (Diogenes), 66.

"It is all ready," etc. (Menander), 72.
"It is for such," etc. (Heraclion), 52.
"It is not," etc. (Isocrates), 59.

Judgment, 7, 18.
   aids in making good poetry, 71.
   altered by good education, 128.
   biased, twists historical narrative, 150.
   bribed by favours, 40.
   formed by philosophy, 59.
   most essential quality, 115.
   of pedants lacking, 92, 93, 98, 99.
   of pupils should be exercised and trained, 12, 13, 33, 34, 92, 93, 96.
   preferred by Plutarch to knowledge, 44.
   questions to try natural, 20.
   should be exercised in showing affection for children, 113, 114.
   teaches to acknowledge error, 40.
   trained by the study of history, 149, 150.
Justice requires conscience, 116.
   taught by the Persians, 105.

Knowledge, acquisition of, 7.
   an ornament to the well-born, 26.
   bookish, useless, 14, 18, 33, 34, 58, 59, 66, 85, 97, 98, 139, 140.
   bought, 94; note 103.
   directs, but can not furnish the mind, 102, 103.
   excessive pursuit of, condemned, 58, 59, 85, 86, 87.
   improperly used is of no value, 139, 140.
   less necessary than judgment, 99.
   little, needed to live well, 131–133.

Knowledge, mendicant, useless, 95.
  must be assimilated, 31, 32, 95, 96.
  noblest, is how to obey and to command, 107.
  of cause and effect is best, 106.
  of nature most sublime, 143.
  practical, should be taught, 49, 50, 92, 97, 98.
  tends to the service of life, 39, 96.
  that is worth most, 11.
Know thyself, 43.

"Labor callum," etc. (Cicero), 36.
Language, Gaza's principle concerning, note 37.
  Greek, 79, 96, 97.
  imitation of, easy, 75, 76.
  in learning a foreign, associate as much as possible with each word, note 37.
  Latin, 77–79, 96, 97.
  Locke's governess of, note 86.
  modern, should be taught first, 11.
  of country people suited to philosophy, 128, 129.
  should be learned in the country where it is spoken, 16.
  should be simple and unaffected, 75.
  vernacular first, 14, 76.
Latin insufficient to educate, 67, 68, 96, 97.
  Montaigne's method of learning, 76, 77.
  Latinist has no practical knowledge, 67.
  should be taught after vernacular, 14, 76.
Law, Montaigne studies, 2–3.
  course of, 19.
Learning an ornament to the well-born, 26.

Learning, better learned preferable to more learned, 92.
  least learned nations the most warlike, 108, 109.
  little, needed to live well, 131–133.
  literal, not enough for a tutor, 28.
  make, alluring and permanent, 85.
  may be applied to evil, 103, 104.
  may be gained from everyone, 41, 42.
  must be assimilated, 31, 32, 95, 96.
  not the true end of education, 128.
  of pedants pretentious, 96–98.
  present, only makes wise, 92, 93.
  that one can not express is useless, 68–70.
  useless if it does not impress the mind, 141, 142.
  useless if without understanding, 101.
  women require little, 101; note 118.
  word, condemned, 29, 30, 83, 97, 98.
Learn to do by doing, 10, 18, 33, 34, 66–68.
Lehrplan of 1892, 8.
"Les faits changent" (Rousseau), note 159.
"Lettre-ferita," 97.
"Licet sapere," etc. (Seneca), 38.
Literature, means of placing a child in relation to his environment, 7.
  sound, should fill minds, 97.
  the tale should be given the child first, 81, 82; note 88.
Logic does not teach effective expression, 138, 139.
  inferior to knowledge, 107.
  logician is no gentleman, 67.

GENERAL INDEX.

Logic not much taught by Aristotle, 57.
subtleties of, condemned, 39, 57.
Luxury should be avoided in bringing up children, 145.
Lying, almost ineradicable, 121.
hateful vice, 122, 123.
national (French) fault, 122, 123.
should be early corrected in children, 121.
the first feature in corruption, 122.
"Lying and perjury" (Massiliensis), 122.

"Magis, magnos clericos," etc. (Rabelais), 87.
"Magna pars libertatis," etc. (Seneca), 145.
"Mais ie hay," etc. (Du Bellay), 86.
Manner, affability of, required of Montaigne, 82.
altered by education, 128.
avoid singularity of, 63, 64.
of speaking and writing should be natural, 73, 74.
Manners of country people suited to philosophy, 128, 129.
preferred to pedantry, 28.
should be observed, 41.
should be trained, 61.
should not be spoiled by association, 58.
should not be too formal, 87, 88; note 20.
Memorizing, arraignment of mere, 18, 29, 30, 33, 34, 92, 95; note 105.
inferior to practice, 66, 67, 105, 106.
not the aim of history, 42.
not true knowledge, 139, 140.
pedantic, 73; note 91.
Methods should be varied, 11.

Millennium not reached through any single revolution, 10.
Mind dilates the more it fills, 87.
requires occupation, 141, 142.
"Μισῶ σοφιστὴν" etc. (Euripides), 95.
Moderation, mankind incapable of, 131.
Montaigne, ability to detect difference between himself and the wise, 21.
antiquity of, ideas, 13.
approves of the stage, 84, 85.
awakened by music, 79.
breadth of view, 12.
brought up among the common people, 145, 146.
clear judgment, 83.
coincidence of opinion with those of others, 21.
comments on his own book, 110.
compares himself to good authors, 21.
disposition, 80, 81.
early education, 77–80.
extols Mme. D'Estissac as a model mother, 111, 112.
family relations, 119, 120.
fancy and judgment uncertain, 20, 21.
first to break away from Renaissance ideals, note 105.
first to develop a connected system of education, 13.
fondness for poetry, 20.
fondness for tales, 81, 82.
founder of a school of thinkers, xv.
history his chief study, 20.
how, was taught Greek and Latin, 77–79.
in advance of his own age and of the present, 7, 10, 11.
ideas on history, 147–152.

Montaigne's inaction, 80, 81, 83.
   indebtedness to other authors, 93.
   lack of formal knowledge, 19, 20.
   lack of memory, 20, 80, 93.
   life of, 1–6.
   modernity, 10.
   natural faculties indifferent, 20, 80, 82.
   never read books of solid learning, 20.
   part in college theatricals, 84.
   slight discipline of his daughter, 116.
   trained against special tastes, 63, 64.
   trained to affability of manner, 82.
   trained to honesty and sincerity, 125, 126.
   use of quotations, 23.
   uses the language of the people, 75.
Morality of life independent of learning, 132, 133.
Moral training, importance of, 123; note 120.
   neglected by pedants, 96, 97.
Motor side, 10, 15, 79.
"Multum interest," etc. (Seneca), 64.
Music, recommended by Plato, 63.
   used to awaken Montaigne, 79.
   musicians ridiculed by Dionysius, 96.

Nature should be the basis of philosophy, 143.
   should yield to authority, 112.
   studies place child in relation to physical environment, 7.
"Nec ad melius," etc. (Cicero), 138.
"Neither the youngest," etc. (Epicurus), 58.

"Neque, ut omnia," etc. (Cicero), 39.
"Nequid quam sapere," etc. (Cicero), 96.
"Non enim paranda," etc. (Cicero), 96.
"Non est loquendum," etc. (Seneca), 93.
"Non sumus sub rege," etc. (Seneca), 31.
"Non vitæ, etc. (Seneca), 101.
"Not to learn logic," etc. (Agesilaus), 107.
"Nullum scelus," etc. (Livy), 117.
"Nunquam tutelæ," etc. (Seneca), 30.
Nuts, anecdote of play with, 124; note 132.

"Obest plerumque," etc. (Cicero), 28.
Observation commended, 41.
Obstinacy increased by whipping, 116.
   should be repressed, 121.
"Odi homines," etc. (Pacuvius), 82.
"Of Athens," "Of the World" (Socrates), 44.
"Omnis Aristippum," etc. (Horace), 65.
Orations, inferior to simple statements, 70, 71.
   not suitable to feasts, 59, 60.
   orators ridiculed by Dionysius, 96.
"Ὃς οἶδεν," etc. (Stobæus), 100.
"O stranger!" etc. (Alexandrides), 44.
"O what," etc. (Seneca), 92.

Patriotism should be instilled, 39, 40.

GENERAL INDEX. 187

"Paucis opus est," etc. (Seneca), 133.
Pedantry, despised by ancients, 86, 87.
  discountenanced, iii–xiv, 30, 58, 59.
  ridiculed, 68.
Pedants, ancient and modern, contrasted, 89.
  lack business ability, 90–92.
  lack judgment, 99.
  neglect moral training, 92, 93.
  pretenders of learning, 97, 98.
  ridiculed, 98, 99.
"Petite hinc," etc. (Persius), 58.
Philosophy, adapted to earliest instruction, 106.
  adapted to festive occasions, 60.
  aims at virtue, 52.
  ancient philosophers contrasted with modern, 89.
  ancient philosophers scorned material circumstances, 87–89.
  ancient philosophers were great in action, 90, 91.
  best suited to vernacular, 128, 129.
  can be applied to evil, 103, 104.
  chief study, 59.
  discourses of, cheer, 51–53.
  examples of, in relation to life, 47, 48.
  gracious to the well-born, 26.
  ignorance of its votaries, note 93.
  not mechanical reading and learning, 66, 67.
  Plato's definition of, 33.
  should be based on nature, 143.
  Tasso's idea of, 26.
  teaches how to live, 55, 66, 67.
"Philosophy is a rich," etc. (Tasso), 26.
Physical training, a modern purpose, 7, 18; note 53.
  "hardening process," note 19.

Physical training, importance of, 16, 36, 37.
  increased attention to, at present, note 53.
  not to be interfered with through mistaken affection, 35, 36.
  recommended by Plato, 61, 62.
  to guard against effeminacy, 62.
Physics, 7, 50.
Plagiarism, assimilated borrowed material may be used, 81, 82.
Play, Dr. Tsanoff's idea of the importance of, in education, note 141.
  Groos upon, of animals, note 141.
  Haddon upon the origin of, note 141.
  Kindergarten, of the sixteenth century, note 141.
  Montaigne advocates, in education, 10.
  of children their most serious actions, 125, 126.
  of great importance and must be without cheating, 125, 126.
  recommended by Plato, 62.
  use of the motor-side in educational games, 15, 79.
Pleasure more toilsome than wisdom, 54.
"Plus sapit vulgus," etc. (Lactantius), 129.
"Plus sonat," etc. (Seneca), 72.
Poetry, Cicero no leisure to study lyric poets, 57.
  despised by Spartans, 107.
  diversion proper for women, note 118.
  good matter makes good, 71, 72.
  Montaigne fond of, 20.
  poetical form aids understanding, 20.
  poetic license should be used by great poets only, 88.

188   THE EDUCATION OF CHILDREN.

Poetry, poets have always accommodated themselves to public feeling, 54.
  recommended by Plato on account of music, 62.
Politician has knowledge of human nature, 3.
"Postquam docti," etc. (Seneca), 102.
Practical life, children should be trained to like ordinary things, 144, 145.
  education used in, 100, 101.
  Persians trained for, 104–106.
  relation of philosophical examples to, 47–50.
  train for, 17, 57, 58, 91, 92, 95, 96, 98, 100.
Process, fitting, narrowing, 3.
Profit, learning should not be for business, 84, 85.
Prognostics, childish, 11, 25.
Propensity of children's minds to be taken into account, 25, 28, 29, 56.
Punishment condemned by Erasmus, note 54.
  often due to anger and unjust, 134, 135.
  makes children more cowardly, wilful, and obstinate, 97.
  severity of, condemned by Locke and Rousseau, 17.
  should be deliberate and discreet, 136, 137.
  youths corrupted by, 62.
Pupils are like masters, 93.

"Quae tellus," etc. (Propertius), 42.
"Quae veritati," etc. (Seneca), 75.
"Queis arte," etc. (Juvenal), 100.
"Quem duplici" (Horace), 65.
"Qui alicujus," etc. (Seneca), 73.

"Quid fas optare," etc. (Persius), 47.
"Qui disciplinam," (Cicero), 67.
"Quid moveant Pisces," etc. (Propertius), 49.
"Quis accurate," etc. (Seneca), 75.
"Quisquis ubique," etc. (Martial), 142.
Quotation, abuse of, 21–23.
  Montaigne's use of, for better self-expression, 23.
Quotations different in various editions of Montaigne, note 4.
"Quum res animum," etc. (Seneca), 69.

"Rabie jecur incendente," etc. (Juvenal), 135.
Reason alone should control inclinations, 113.
  common property, 31.
  should be chief guide, 40.
Reflection, children's power of, note 46.
Religion, Christian, requires little learning in women, 101.
  influence on Greeks of free, 5.
  Montaigne's attitude toward, 5.
  new, 10.
  thought, 9.
"Reserve these tricks," etc. (Chrysippus), 73.
Rhetoric, 33.
  does not teach effective expression, 70, 71, 138, 139.
  inferior to knowledge, 106, 107.
Rhetorical disputes not suited to feasts, 60.
Rights, children's, 113, 114.

"Sapere aude," etc. (Horace), 49.
School, make, life pleasant, 11, 17, 18.

School, make, pleasant through variety, 50, 51.
should not inflict punishment, 61, 62, 85.
should not represent study difficult, 51, 52.
Schools do not produce great men, 8, 96, 97.
Self-activity, 11, 12.
Self-consciousness to be avoided, 45, 46, 63.
" Si cupidus," etc. (Juvenal), 96.
Silence, train children to, 37, 38.
Similarity, striking verbal, of Montaigne, Locke, and Rousseau, 14.
Simplicity commended, 130, 131.
taught by Socrates, 130, 131.
Sincerity requires acknowledgment of errors, 40.
" Si quid Socrates," etc. (Cicero), 88.
Sound mind in a sound body, 11, 36, 52, 61.
Spectators, inactive, of life not the worst men, 47.
Speculation of Thales, 91; note 99.
Spoiling children, 35-37.
Stage approved by Montaigne, 84, 85.
should be encouraged by the government, 85.
State education, 184, 145.
Sternness repented of, 118, 119.
Study, do not make, distasteful through punishment, 61, 62.
do not represent, as difficult, 51, 52.
excessive, injurious, 20, 58, 59, 87.
in France aims at profit, 101, 102.
make, pleasant, 61, 85 ; note 87.
nature, 7.
political, 7.
should make wiser, 32, 33.

Study, should not aim at business profit, 101, 102.
should, to live, 66, 67.
sociological, 7.
time and place of, immaterial, 59.
Style should be simple and harmonize with matter, 73, 74.
" Sub aliena umbra," etc. (Seneca), 139.
Subtleties of logic condemned, 39, 57; note 40.
of sophistries laughable, 72, 73.
Susceptibility of everyone to education, 128 ; note 45.

Tabular form of similar passages from Locke, Montaigne, and Rousseau, 15-17.
Tale, value of the, in early education, 81, 82 ; note 88.
Teacher apt to be narrow, 8.
care in choice of a, 11, 28.
Tel fiert quo no tue pas, note 1.
" Tempora certa," etc. (Horace), 71.
Tête bien faite, 8.
" The gods forbid," etc. (Plato), 66.
" The inhabitants of Asia," etc. (Plutarch), 43.
Theories, modernity of the, of Erasmus, Rabelais, Montaigne, xv.
" The poor boy," etc. (Marshal de Montluc), 119.
Things before words, 10, 18, 68-76, 144.
Thought, imitation of, difficult, 75, 76.
richness of, better than fertility of speech, 76.
" Till our armies," etc. (Crates), 90.
" Τί πλείδεσσι," etc. (Anacreon, 49.
" To what purpose," etc. (Anaximenes), 50.
Translation of Montaigne, xv, xvi.

Travel, broadening influence of, 44–47.
  importance of, 11, 18, 34, 35.
  Montaigne's account of his, 4; note 15.
Truth, banishment of, the first feature of corruption, 122.
  common property, 31, 32.
  has only one face, 122.
  language of, plain and unaffected, 75.
  moral truths connected with modern educational methods, note 144.
  simple truth better than many words, 70, 71.
  train children to speak the, 121.
Tutor, authority of, should be sovereign, 37.
  choice of, most important, 11, 14, 15, 18, 29.
  Montaigne's, very discreet, 82.
  powers of a, note 43.
  should be a gentleman, 28, note 8.
  should inculcate affection as well as reverence for virtue, 54.
  should train pupil's judgment, 28, 29.

"Udum et molle," etc. (Persius), 56.
Understanding, fundamental requirement for learning, 101.
  rules all, according to Epicharmus, 32.
Usefulness, training for, 7, 17, 18, 49, 57, 58.
"Ut fuerit melius," etc. (Cicero), 101.
Utile, 112, 113.
"Ut omnium rerum" (Seneca), 131.

Vanity, Locke speaks against, note 140.
"Velut ægri somnia," etc. (Horace), 141.
"Verbaque provisam," etc. (Horace), 69.
Vernacular, first, 14, 76.
  suited to philosophy, 128, 129.
Versatility, commended, 64, 65.
  of Alcibiades, 65.
Vices, abhorrence of, should be taught, 124, 125.
Violence, physical, in discipline condemned, 61, 62, 116, 135, 137.
Virtue, fundamental, 102.
  of fathers should hold children, 115.
  practice of, pleasant, 52, 55.
  seen in the actions of men, 66, 67.
  should be inculcated, 92, 127.
  taught by the Persians, 104, 105.
  value of, 54, 55.
Virtues, great, gain privileges, 33.
  should be shown in speech, 40.
  taught by Aristotle rather than sciences, 57, 58.
"Vitamque sub," etc. (Horace), 35.
"Vos O patricius," etc. (Persius), 99.

Wars, little mischief done by, 45.
Wealth, a provision against neglect in old age, 115.
"We have," etc. (Cato), 71.
"What a stupid," etc. (Socrates), 107.
"What they ought," etc. (Agesilaus), 106.
Whipping, condemned, 97.
  of Cyrus for a wrong judgment, 105, 106.
  often due to anger, 135, 136.

GENERAL INDEX.

Whipping, Latin learned without, 78.
Whole, knowledge of the, necessary to true valuation of the parts, 45, 46.
— man must be trained, 60, 61.
"Why should I," etc. (Aristippus), 73.
Will, restrain, within limits, 64.
Wisdom, brought to earth by Socrates, 130.
— gained from nature, 143.
— less toilsome than pleasure, 54.
— not gained by logic, 138, 139.

Wisdom of fathers should hold children, 115.
— sign of, is cheerfulness, 52, 53.
Wit never out of place, 71.
Women, do not require much learning, 101.
— Montaigne's view of, note 16.
— take part in physical contests, note 57.
— what, should learn, note 118.
World, the best text-book, 46, 47.

"You are," etc. (Diogenes), 66.

THE END.

D. APPLETON AND COMPANY'S PUBLICATIONS.

New Volumes in the International Education Series.

BIBLIOGRAPHY OF EDUCATION. By Will S. Monroe, A. B., Department of Pedagogy and Psychology, State Normal School, Westfield, Mass. $2.00.

This book will prove of great use to normal schools, training schools for teachers, and to educational lecturers and all special students seeking to acquaint themselves with the literature of any particular department. It will be of especial value to librarians in the way of assisting them to answer two questions : (*a*) What books has this library on any special educational theme ? (*b*) What books ought it to obtain to complete its collection in that theme ?

FROEBEL'S EDUCATIONAL LAWS FOR ALL TEACHERS. By James L. Hughes, Inspector of Schools, Toronto. $1.50.

The aim of this book is to give a simple exposition of the most important principles of Froebel's educational philosophy, and to make suggestions regarding the application of these principles to the work of the schoolroom in teaching and training. It will answer the question often propounded, How far beyond the kindergarten can Froebel's principles be successfully applied ?

SCHOOL MANAGEMENT AND SCHOOL METHODS. By Dr. J. Baldwin, Professor of Pedagogy in the University of Texas ; Author of "Elementary Psychology and Education" and "Psychology applied to the Art of Teaching." $1.50.

This is eminently an everyday working book for teachers; practical, suggestive, inspiring. It presents clearly the best things achieved, and points the way to better things. School organization, school control, and school methods are studies anew from the standpoint of pupil betterment. The teacher is led to create the ideal school, embodying all that is best in school work, and stimulated to endeavor earnestly to realize the ideal.

PRINCIPLES AND PRACTICE OF TEACHING. By James Johonnot. Revised by Sarah Evans Johonnot. $1.50

This book embodies in a compact form the results of the wide experience and careful reflection of an enthusiastic teacher and school supervisor. Mr. Johonnot as an educational reformer helped thousands of struggling teachers who had brought over the rural school methods into village school work. He made life worth living to them. His help, through the pages of this book, will aid other thousands in the same struggle to adopt the better methods that are possible in the graded school. The teacher who aspires to better his instruction will read this book with profit.

D. APPLETON AND COMPANY, NEW YORK.

D. APPLETON AND COMPANY'S PUBLICATIONS.

JAMES SULLY'S WORKS.

STUDIES OF CHILDHOOD. 8vo. Cloth, $2.50.

An ideal popular scientific book. These studies proceed on sound scientific lines in accounting for the mental manifestations of children, yet they require the reader to follow no laborious train of reasoning; and the reader who is in search of entertainment merely will find it in the quaint sayings and doings with which the volume abounds.

CHILDREN'S WAYS. Being Selections from the Author's "Studies of Childhood," and some additional matter. 12mo. Cloth, $1.50.

This work is mainly a condensation of the author's previous book, "Studies of Childhood," but considerable new matter is added. The material that Mr. Sully supplies is the most valuable of recent contributions on the psychological phases of child study.

TEACHER'S HAND-BOOK OF PSYCHOLOGY. On the Basis of "Outlines of Psychology." Abridged by the Author for the use of Teachers, Schools, Reading Circles, and Students generally. Fourth edition, rewritten and enlarged. 12mo. Cloth, $1.50.

The present edition has been carefully revised throughout, largely rewritten, and enlarged by about fifty pages. While seeking to preserve the original character of the book as an *introduction*, I have felt it necessary, in view of the fact that our best training colleges for secondary teachers are now making a serious study of psychology, to amplify somewhat and bring up to date the exposition of scientific principles. I have also touched upon those recent developments of experimental psychology which have concerned themselves with the measurement of the simpler mental processes, and which promise to have important educational results by supplying accurate tests of children's abilities."—*From the Author's Preface.*

OUTLINES OF PSYCHOLOGY, with Special Reference to the Theory of Education. A Text-Book for Colleges. Crown 8vo. Cloth, $3.00.

ILLUSIONS. A Psychological Study. 12mo, 372 pages. Cloth, $1.50.

PESSIMISM. A History and a Criticism. Second edition. 8vo, 470 pages and Index. Cloth, $4.00.

THE HUMAN MIND. A Text-Book of Psychology. Two volumes. 8vo. Cloth, $5.00.

D. APPLETON AND COMPANY, NEW YORK.

D. APPLETON & CO.'S PUBLICATIONS.

BOYS IN THE MOUNTAINS AND ON THE PLAINS; or, *The Western Adventures of Tom Smart, Bob Edge, and Peter Small.* By W. H. RIDEING, Member of the Geographical Surveys under Lieutenant Wheeler. With 101 Illustrations. Square 8vo. Cloth, gilt side and back, $2.50.

"A handsome gift-book relating to travel, adventure, and field sports in the West." —*New York Times.*

"Mr. Rideing's book is intended for the edification of advanced young readers. It narrates the adventures of Tom Smart, Bob Edge, and Peter Small, in their travels through the mountainous region of the West, principally in Colorado. The author was a member of the Wheeler expedition, engaged in surveying the Territories, and his descriptions of scenery, mining life, the Indians, games, etc., are in a great measure derived from personal observation and experience. The volume is handsomely illustrated, and can not but prove attractive to young readers."—*Chicago Journal.*

BOYS COASTWISE; or, All Along the Shore. By W. H. RIDEING. Uniform with "Boys in the Mountains." With numerous Illustrations. Illuminated boards, $1.75.

"Fully equal to the best of the year's holiday books for boys. . . . In his present trip the author takes them among scenes of the greatest interest to all boys, whether residents on the coast or inland—along the wharves of the metropolis, aboard the pilot-boats for a cruise, with a look at the great ocean steamers, among the life-saving men, coast wreckers and divers, and finally on a tour of inspection of lighthouses and light-ships, and other interesting phases of nautical and coast life."—*Christian Union.*

THE CRYSTAL HUNTERS. A Boy's Adventures in the Higher Alps. By GEORGE MANVILLE FENN, author of "In the King's Name," "Dick o' the Fens," etc. 12mo. Cloth, $1.50.

"This is the boys' favorite author, and of the many books Mr. Fenn has written for them this will please them the best. While it will not come under the head of sensational, it is yet full of life and of those stirring adventures which boys always delight in."—*Christian at Work.*

"English pluck and Swiss coolness are tested to the utmost in these perilous explorations among the higher Alps, and quite as thrilling as any of the narrow escapes is the account of the first breathless ascent of a real mountain-peak. It matters little to the reader whether the search for crystals is rewarded or not, so concerned does he become for the fate of the hunters."—*Literary World.*

SYD BELTON: The Boy who would not go to Sea. By GEORGE MANVILLE FENN. With 6 full-page Illustrations. 12mo. Cloth, $1.50.

"Who among the young story-reading public will not rejoice at the sight of the old combination, so often proved admirable—a story by Manville Fenn, illustrated by Gordon Browne? The story, too, is one of the good old sort, full of life and vigor, breeziness and fun. It begins well and goes on better, and from the time Syd joins his ship, exciting incidents follow each other in such rapid and brilliant succession that nothing short of absolute compulsion would induce the reader to lay it down."—*London Journal of Education.*

D. APPLETON AND COMPANY, NEW YORK.

BOOKS BY HEZEKIAH BUTTERWORTH.
Uniform Edition. Each, 12mo, cloth, $1.50.

The Story of Magellan. Illustrated.
Of the many dramatic chapters of the romantic decades of discovery in the fifteenth and sixteenth centuries, The Story of Magellan yields to none in picturesqueness and heroic quality. Mr. Butterworth's story of the conditions preceding Magellan's expedition, of the adventures of the voyage, the discovery of the Philippines, and the completion of the first circumnavigation of the globe, records the facts of history which are in themselves more wonderful and engrossing than any fiction. In addition to the artists' illustrations, various maps, portraits, and pictures of places increase the historical value of this instructive book.

The Pilot of the Mayflower.
Illustrated by H. Winthrop Peirce and Others.

True to his Home.
A Tale of the Boyhood of Franklin. Illustrated by H. Winthrop Peirce.

The Wampum Belt;
Or, *The Fairest Page of History.* A Tale of William Penn's Treaty with the Indians. With 6 full-page Illustrations.

The Knight of Liberty.
A Tale of the Fortunes of Lafayette. With 6 full-page Illustrations.

The Patriot Schoolmaster.
A Tale of the Minutemen and the Sons of Liberty. With 6 full-page Illustrations by H. Winthrop Peirce.

In the Boyhood of Lincoln.
A Story of the Black Hawk War and the Tunker Schoolmaster. With 12 Illustrations and colored Frontispiece.

The Boys of Greenway Court.
A Story of the Early Years of Washington. With 10 full-page Illustrations.

The Log School-House on the Columbia.
With 13 full-page Illustrations by J. Carter Beard, E. J. Austen, and Others.

D. APPLETON AND COMPANY, NEW YORK.

www.ingramcontent.com/pod-product-compliance
Lightning Source LLC
Chambersburg PA
CBHW021838230426
43669CB00008B/1010